Condo Living Dallas

By Ryan Shea

214-552-9304
ryanshea22@gmail.com

Condo Living Dallas / Ryan Shea

ISBN-13: 9781794180659

Contents

Foreword

There is no one that I know who is better fit to write about condo living — in Dallas or most anywhere — than Ryan Shea! He is in the top 1% of producing real estate Agents in America and is so because of His kind, authentic and caring essence...not to mention His vast knowledge of real estate and specifically condominiums.

This is a very unique book in that it can help everyone who is seeking to have an improved lifestyle with condominium living, while helping other real estate Agents learn from Him...Ryan is considered the Agent of Agents!

Ryan also helps anyone seeking a new career in real estate and helps Agents who are seeking more service to Others, more income and wealth! He has perfected the condo buying and selling experience that exceeds the customer's expectations while helping Agents turn from a sales person to an Experienced Expert.

Ryan is a BIG believer in experiencing the American Dream and is a master at understanding Others and this book will help You get more of what You want!

Soak up the knowledge contained in this book and find a new way to live Your Life with more freedom, more abundance and the secrets that Ryan shares with You 💐

Dr. Hank
Agent Wealth Network

Chapter 1 – The Condominium Lifestyle Thrives in Dallas

Maybe you have admired the thriving new high-rises in the Harwood district The Blue Ciel and The Azzure, or maybe the high-rises in Victory Park The W and The House, or the Arts District high-rises of the One Arts Plaza or the Museum Tower. Perhaps you know someone who lives in a townhome condominium and envy their carefree lifestyle. It could be you just want to simplify your life. Whatever your motivation, you'll find attractive options in Dallas! In fact, there has never been a better time to consider condominium living.

Back to Dallas's Future

To understand where the condominium market is going, it helps to learn where it came from. The story of Dallas's evolving residential landscape follows the changing demographics of other major American cities.

Before World War II (1939), American cities thrived with busy commercial streets, lively sidewalk traffic, and strong vibrant downtowns. The negative effects of industrialization, with its smoke and pollution, noise and crowding, increasing crime rates and poverty, began to push people out of city centers. Suburban life became a reality for many Americans, thanks to the evolution of public transportation and the accelerated pace of automobile production after World War II.

Downtowns that were once the center of excitement became the place not to be. For the next 60 years, suburban developments were touted as retreats from city centers. Eventually people were able to work, live, play, and shop in suburbs while life in the inner cities became stagnant. This suburban crawl crept across America for decades, thanks to the aggressive marketing of the American Dream.

"I look forward to an America which will not be afraid of grace and beauty, which will protect the beauty of our natural environment, which will preserve the great old American houses and squares and parks of our national past and which will build handsome and balanced cities for our future."

-John F Kennedy, 35th President of the United States of America

In that Dream, prospective home buyers stood on perfect lots in suburban subdivisions enjoying views of woodlands, farmlands, and wildlife. Over a handful of years however, the scenery started to change. The deer were gone, woodlands were bulldozed, and fields were covered with new concrete streets.

Of course, a person could have moved every few years and stayed ahead of the developments under construction, but that is not realistic. All this development caused traffic congestion, creating longer commutes and less time at home for suburbanites.

Suburbanites learned that living the American Dream of getting away from city life came with a price. That price is now being re-evaluated by the very Americans who've spent most of their lives in the suburbs.

I am not anti-suburbia. In fact, there are many condominium developments being built in the far-reaching suburbs as I write this. I grew up outside of town in the suburbs. So playing soccer, baseball, flashlight tag in the fields, and riding bikes through the neighborhood were a way of life for me growing up. These are all amazing memories for me.

This population spread across America's landscape and caused a vacuum in our inner cities leaving vacant buildings, abandoned warehouses, and dirty vacant lots that littered the landscape.

Urban Renaissance

The solution to balancing today's large cities with the surrounding countryside is to develop these underutilized urban areas. In Dallas some of the areas that have been transformed in recent years were the Victory Park area, the Design District, and the Trinity River Project. These areas were once covered by warehouse buildings. By offering tax, economic, financial, and regulatory incentives, cities have been able to attract developers in a nationwide mission to revive inner cities.

You may not have realized it, but this renaissance of American cities is great news! It's bringing back an exciting lifestyle that has not been experienced since the early 1900's. Cities are developing large condominium projects and surrounding them with sports venues, grocery stores, movie theatres, restaurants, art galleries, urban gardens, running, walking, bike trails, parks, performing arts centers and much more. There is a combination of revitalized buildings and new condominium buildings to bring strong character and variety to these new full-service urban neighborhoods.

Dallas Boom

Following the market crash of 2007-2008 Dallas has made a strong comeback with many developments currently under construction or beginning. Several developments such as Museum Tower, Harwood district, Klyde Warren Park, and Dallas Themed Bridges like the Margaret Hunt bridge have just recently finished with units still available for sale.

Region Plush With Culture

Dallas for good or bad has been called a mini Los Angeles.

Dallas has all the major sports franchises: the Dallas Cowboys in the National Football League, Dallas Mavericks in the National Basketball Association, Texas Rangers in Major League Baseball, Dallas Stars in the National Hockey Association, and FC Dallas in Major League Soccer. It is also home to Double AA affiliates of the Texas Rangers, Frisco Rough Riders, and home to Lone Star Park in Grand Prairie. Dallas has hosted the Super Bowl, National Football championship, and the final four.

Dallas is home to the Dallas Opera and Symphony. The 12th annual film festival, hosted by the Dallas Film Society, was just held this past May 2018 in Dallas. The Dallas area attracts some of the largest and best celebrities to perform at The American Airlines Center, Jerry's world.

Dallas offers designer shopping and has always been known as a shopping headquarters and destination with the Design District annual shop to you drop week.

Affordable Living

Dallas's low taxes make it a destination for both individuals looking to turn a new leaf on life and businesses. Texas has no state income tax, and while Texas property taxes are sometimes considered high by outsiders, Dallas still ranks as one of the top five cities in terms of tax rate.

The city of Dallas has done a great job of attracting and promoting the business advantages of Dallas Fort Worth. Recently, there has been talk of Amazon's HQ2 headquarters here in the DFW area. Some companies who have moved to the DFW area in the recent months and years are Toyota, FED Ex Headquarters, and Jamba Juice, just to name a few.

Another reason for this growth is the median price range of the residential real estate as compared to other parts of the country. The cost of living in Dallas Fort Worth as compared to the rest of the country is second to none. However, prices have started to rise as a result of demand and so many businesses moving here it attracts and has been attracting a population increase.

The current development in DFW and surrounding areas has been nothing short of spectacular. There are not too many places in and around downtown Dallas that you will not see our current state logo, the construction crane ☺. Even when the market crashed in 2007-2008 activity remained strong for construction and real estate comparatively speaking. However, one of the hardest hit markets was the condominium market. Many of these areas that were hard hit have made a resurgence and are coming back strong. Victory Park is a good example of this resurgence. It is brimming with new retail, restaurants, movie theatre, thousands of new apartments, and also thousands of new office and commercial spaces.

Dallas' attention on the national stage has been super helpful to attract businesses from far and wide. Dallas is regularly in the Top 10 of best and most affordable places to move in the country. With an estimated 300 people a week moving to the DFW metroplex it is certainly one of the hottest real estate markets in the country. Dallas was the 3rd fastest growing city in 2014 and 146,000 residents moved to DFW in 2017. The metroplex has great accessibility with 2 centralized airports: Love Field and DFW International Airport. Love Field is the home to Southwest Airlines and is just minutes from Downtown Dallas. DFW International is the home base for American Airlines and has just went through a Billion Dollar renovation and addition. Yes, that is Billion with a "B".

Redevelopment and building have pushed the Dallas Metroplex market in the front stage With New York City, Los Angeles, and Miami. Looking over the rich history of oil, business, ecommerce, expansion, growth, cost effectiveness, Dallas is here to stay as on one of the Best places to be in America today.

> "We're Texas, maybe for the rest of the country, it's as good as it gets, but Texas has a lot of things going for it. When I go to work, all I see are positives. I see happy clients, I see deal flow, and I see more and more companies moving into the great state of Texas."
>
> *- Ross Perot Jr., Real Estate Developer*

Dallas's evolving urban experience is very similar to other American cities. Dallas has been on the cutting edge of development since condominiums were first developed in the 60's. The oil boom of the 1970's and 1980's gave rise to many of the high-rise buildings in downtown Dallas. Within the past few years of development during the downturn in the economy with W and the House in Victory Park, as well as the One Art's Plaza, The Ritz Carlton Residences, The Azzurre in Harwood district. More recent developments include the Blue Ciel in Harwood, The Museum Tower, Corvella at Stonebriar in Frisco, Hall arts Residences, Parkside overlooking Klyde Warren Park, Residences at Stoneleigh, and Windrose Tower in Plano just to name a few of the condominium and townhome developments in and around the Dallas-Ft. Worth market.

Dallas and Texas are becoming second to none in developments and especially residential condominium high-rises and mid-rises, as well as townhome developments. Currently, Dallas is in a major expansive stage which started in 2005 with the development of Victory Park, then the market crashed with the Real Estate and lending crisis. However, in recent years the downtown areas of Dallas and surrounding areas have seen a major resurgence with the above-mentioned condo developments.

Communities

Urban Dallas

Downtown Dallas has a lot to offer and has been the focal point of making downtown Dallas a comfortable, fun destination. Within the past 15 years some notable changes, improvements, and additions have been made. Klyde Warren Park was built above Woodall Rogers Freeway. The additions of the The Museum Tower and Parkside Condos and the new development Hall Arts Residences have given the downtown area a boost in downtown high-rise condominiums. Downtown Dallas has expanded to include Victory Park north to the Ritz and the Harwood district of the Azurre and Bleu Ciel.

The downtown area is easily accessible by car, bus, train, and trolley. The trolley runs from the West Village to downtown near Klyde Warren Park. The Dart, which goes right through the heart of downtown, has access to the DFW International airport, Victory Park and the American Airlines Center.

This surge in interest in the downtown Dallas is due in large part to the successful growth and development of the surrounding neighborhoods and what has become downtown Dallas such as Victory Park, The Harwood district, The Arts District, Uptown, Parkland Hospital area, along with the numerous residential properties that have boosted the popularity and viability of living in downtown Dallas.

Add to the list of successes new hotel facilities at the Omni Hotel and Convention Center, the new addition of the Virgin Hotel in the Design District, and The largest continuous Arts District in the United States including the AT&T Performing Arts Center and Margot and Bill Winspear Opera House, The Hunt Building which is a unique design leading into Downtown Dallas, and other corporate building projects, as well as the Trinity River project with the numerous Bridges the Margaret Hunt Hill

Bridge extending across the Trinity River from Woodall Rogers Park, The Ronald Kirk Pedestrian Bridge, and The Margaret McDermott Bridge that will be the bridge over the Trinity for Interstate 30, and the proposed Harold Simmons Park in the Trinity River corridor near the Design District.

Such dramatic changes in Downtown Dallas have fostered the development of prime residential neighborhoods in previously underused or old industrial buildings where the land value is high. Some of the old buildings are being restored, however most of these sites are being torn down and replaced with newly built condominiums and apartments that blend well and complement the existing urban environment.

> "When you look at a city, it's like reading the hopes, aspirations and pride of everyone who built it."
>
> *- Hugh Newell Jacobsen, Architect*

The success of the condominium market downtown is due to some mental reconditioning. Suburbanites for years have been trained to avoid downtown because it was considered scary, desolate, and no activity.

Thanks to new developments and the already LA type feel of the downtown market, urban energy is strong in downtown Dallas. Add the creativity and dedication of the people of Dallas and you have a growing thriving urban haven, and a one heck of a fun and exciting place.

Currently there are over 70 Condominium/townhome projects in the downtown area with units ranging in sizes from 600 Square feet to 7,000 plus square feet. The properties include Trinity River views, downtown Dallas views, underground parking to street parking, and new construction to old conversions.

To find out more about these new and existing developments please go to www.CondoLivingDallas.com.

Downtown Dallas is continuing to make its mark on the national and world scene. The downtown Dallas market is a model of urban progress, and not just for the central location in the United States. It is continuing to get tremendous attention on the national scene, which is all well deserved. If you would like to know more about Urban Dallas please go to www.CondoLivingDallas.com.

Oak Lawn

The geographical landscape of Oak lawn more than likely depends on who you are talking to. There are varying ideas of where to draw the line. The lines move based on what people remember in their younger years. Unofficially, boundaries are Turtle Creek to Central Expressway (Hwy 75) Highland Park to Inwood and Harry Hines. Officially it is bounded by Highland Park to Central Expressway (Hwy 75) to Stemmons Freeway to Woodall Rogers.

The earliest history of condominiums in Dallas is entrenched in the Oak Lawn/Turtle Creek area. The first of the high-rise condominiums in Dallas is the one and only 3525 Turtle Creek.

Oak Lawn has an estimated population of 50,000 and is one of the wealthier areas in metropolitan Dallas. It is mostly condos, townhomes, apartments – roughly 90% are condominiums or townhomes. However, there are several single-family neighborhoods highlighted by Perry Heights. There are also a few condominiums in that small single-family neighborhood.

Lee park and the Turtle Creek park are two of the most well-known parks and the center of social life in Oak Lawn.

To find out more about the new and existing developments with Oak Lawn please go to www.CondoLivingDallas.com.

Uptown Dallas

Uptown Dallas is one of the more pedestrian friendly parts of Dallas. It is similar to the downtown and Oak Lawn areas in that most of the residences are condominiums and townhomes. Uptown is north of and adjacent to downtown Dallas, and is bordered by US 75 (Central Expressway) on the east, N Haskell Avenue on the northeast, Katy Trail on the northwest, Bookhout Street and Cedar Springs Road on the west, N Akard Street on the southwest and Spur 366 (Woodall Rodgers Freeway) on the south.

Uptown's most trafficked and popular areas are the famed McKinney Ave., West Village, State/Thomas and Knox/Henderson areas. The Katy Trail also runs through the Uptown area and really is the split between Uptown and Oak Lawn. The State Thomas area is one of the highlights of the Uptown area. It has brownstone residential condominiums, townhomes, apartments and retail space. It is approximately 4-5 blocks east to west and 4-5 blocks north to south. One of the more exclusive hotels and residence in Dallas, the Hotel Zaza, is on the border of this amazing State Thomas area. The Metropolitan Club which is the residence adjacent to the Hotel Zaza has all the amenities. There are many restaurants, bars, yoga, and shopping.

The uptown area has usually around 100 active condominiums and townhomes for sale ranging from 1 Bedroom 600 square foot condominiums all the way up to 5000 square foot 3-bedroom Townhomes. There are price points and sizes everywhere in between these two end points. You can get more information on Uptown Dallas condominium projects at www.CondoLivingDallas.com.

Park Cities

Park Cities has its share of condominiums, townhomes, Garden Homes and Single Family Attached (½ Duplex homes). This area is one of the most valuable areas in the whole Dallas Fort Worth Metroplex for its central location, schools, parks, running trails, water, and vegetation. The Park Cities will break down into 4 segments. 1) City of Highland Park and Highland Park Independent School District 2) City of Highland Park and Dallas Independent School District 3) City of University Park and Highland Park Independent School District 4) City of Dallas and Highland Park Independent Schools. So, are you confused yet? I will break each of these areas down and then also focus on the Condominium and Townhome communities within each area.

One of the major attraction points to the Park Cities are the schools which have very high ratings. Plus, it has many parks, retail Highland Park Village, Preston Center, Snider Plaza, Southern Methodist University, Dallas Athletic Club and the always famed Bubba's, and is always known within the Dallas Fort Worth Metroplex as the best Christmas light show on the homes in the area.

City of Highland Park, Highland Park Independent School District, is one of if not the most coveted areas within the Dallas/Fort Worth Metroplex. It's boundaries are on the west the Dallas North Tollway up to Mockingbird to the north (University Park) then it zig zags north and east to Preston and across to the west on McFarlin and then starts south on Golf drive and zig zags south to Mockingbird lane and west to Airline and then south to the Katy Trail to Armstrong lane then zig zags around turtle creek to just north of Hawthorne over to Lemmon and then starts running north with the west Dallas North Tollway Boundary. Or simply approximately 3 miles north of Downtown Dallas! The price ranges from a small 500 plus square foot one-bedroom condo up to nearly 2500 square feet, 2-bedroom, 2 bath, 3 car garage with amenities including concierge service, monitored cameras, business center, guest suite, and underground parking for the Mondara Condos off Abbott. There is every price point in between.

City of Highland Park, Dallas Independent School District which is commonly known as Highland Park West. It has an east border with the Dallas North Tollway, with north border on Mockingbird and South border of Lemmon, west border of Westside drive. This is a smaller portion of Highland Park and does have townhomes on the south west corner Highland Park just north of Lemmon on Westside Drive. The townhomes were built in the early 1980's and range in size from 2600 square feet up to 2,800 square feet, 2 to 3 bedrooms with 2 car garages.

City of University Park, Highland Park Independent School District has south border of Highland Park, west going north border of Dallas North Tollway with a few zig zags up to Greenbriar and starts zig zag northeast up to Northwest Highway via Preston, then goes south on Airline and then zig zags south over to Lovers lane and then there is small jump across US Highway 75, on south to Mockingbird. If that is not clear as mud wait until the City of Dallas, Highland Park ISD! This portion of the Park Cities has the largest number of condominiums, townhomes, Garden Homes, and Single Family Attached Homes that range from midcentury to new construction. The largest portion of these homes are centered around Southern Methodist University. The condominiums range from one-bedroom at around 800 square feet up to a five-bedroom Single Family attached with just under 4,000 square feet, built in 2016. There are two-, three- and four-bedroom condominiums, townhomes, Single Family attached homes ranging in size from around 1,000 square feet up to just under 4,000 square feet.

City of Dallas, Highland Park Independent School District is tough to explain boundaries because of all the zig zag areas on the outside border of Highland and University Park make up the City of Dallas in HPISD. There is one big high-rise condominium in this area, the Shelton Condos. The Shelton Condos were built in 1983 with the south facing condominiums having downtown views. All of The Shelton Condos have Valet Parking, 24-7 front desk, fitness center, clubroom, heated pool, private pool side cabanas, putting green, shuffle board, and covered outdoor grill space. Unit sizes range from 1000 square foot one-bedrooms to 2,800 square foot three-bedrooms. The Charleston Square Condos were built in 1985 and offer an elevator to secured underground parking. The Northpark Garden Townhomes were built in 1964 and are 2-bedroom, 2 story condominiums, ranging from just over 1,200 square feet up to just over 1,500 square feet. There is a community pool and the townhomes are conveniently located on the opposite corner of Northpark Mall.

Preston Hollow

The boundaries of Preston Hollow really depend on who you talk to because there are different boundary lines. The most common boundary is South border of Northwest Highway, North border of Royal Lane, east border of Hillcrest, and west border of Midway. However, a common Area in the Real Estate world is called Area 11, which has a boundary line of South Northwest Highway, East Highway 75 or central expressway, North border of Interstate 635, and west border of Midway. However you determine the boundary, this general area is plush with high end real estate and Stars including George W Bush, Mark Cuban, Jordan Spieth, and T Boone Pickens just to name a few. It is home to the famed North Park Center, which has 2 million square feet of retail shopping, and 235 stores. This is where the who's who of Dallas does their shopping.

The condominium, townhomes and Garden Homes/zero lot lines are plenty in Preston Hollow, with many of the condominiums and townhomes located around the border of Preston Hollow. For example, the Athena and Preston Tower Condo and Sorrento Condo are on the south border with several condominiums on the east side bordering 75, and several condominium complexes on the north side near 635. The Sorrento is a 5 story, 97-unit condominium complex in North Dallas just north of Northwest Highway and just west of Hillcrest. Several of the amenities offered are underground parking, roof top deck, pool and fitness center. There are 1-, 2- and 3-bedroom condos with square footage for a one-bedroom as low as 837 square feet and as large as a two-bedroom unit with 2,340 square feet.

Preston Hollow has several townhome developments. Pagewood townhomes just west of 75 in between Meadow and Royal is an affordable option. These townhomes were built in the early 1970's. There are 2- and 3-bedroom options ranging in square footage from approximately 1,100 square feet up to 1,800 square feet. The Preston Square community is a 250 residential townhome community that was built in the early 1980's. It has a swimming pool, clubhouse, and tennis courts as well as 33 acres of greenbelts within the community. There are 2-, 3-, and 4-bedroom units with 2 car garages. The size of the townhomes ranges from 1,565 square feet up to 2,645 square feet.

There are several neighborhoods that have Garden Home/zero lot lines. Two of those are Glen Lakes and Lake Forest. Glen Lakes is 286 custom home, gated community that has a pool, tennis, running and walking trails, lakes, fountains and lush greenery throughout. Lake Forest is a 68-acre park like gated community with 24-hour security, tennis courts, picnic areas, a swim pavilion, walking and jogging trails, and dog park.

East Dallas

The East Dallas area has several condominiums, townhomes and zero lot line homes. There are several separate communities that I will talk about individually within east Dallas. These areas are Lakewood, M Streets area, Upper Greenville, Deep Ellum, and Lake Highlands, White Rock lake area of east Dallas. East Dallas is a very large area and covers the largest geographical area in Dallas. The general area for east Dallas has an easy west border of 75 or Central Expressway and southern border of Interstate 30 with an east border of Loop 12 going north up to Northwest Highway. Lake Highlands is then North of Northwest Highway with a north border of Interstate 635 and a west border of Highway 75 or Central Expressway.

Deep Ellum has the largest number of condominiums and townhomes in this area and is just east of northeast of Downtown Dallas. With over 30 live music venues Deep Ellum is a center for the arts, restaurants, and business. Deep Ellum is very well known for its restaurant, bar and music scene. It has gone through a major redevelopment in the past number of years while also keeping some of the original structures and allure of days of old.

M Streets area (Lower Greenville) is South of Mockingbird, east of 75, west of Abrams and north of Munger. This has a high concentration of condominiums and townhomes and many newer build condominiums and townhomes. There are one-bedroom condominiums for $150,000 all the way up to the million-dollar price point for a three-bedroom at the Realty America Hotel. The M Streets is a desired destination point because of its neighborhood restaurants, nightlife, parks, location to downtown, and accessibility to the Dart Train at Mockingbird Station and the Katy Trail.

Lakewood has a north boundary of Mockingbird White Rock Lake as an east boundary, Abrams as a west boundary and the south boundary is Gaston. Lakewood is well known for its top-rated elementary school Lakewood Elementary. Of course, it is known for White Rock Lake which has been a biking, running, dog park, park area for many, many generations of Dallas families. There are several condo and townhome neighborhoods ranging in the low $200,000 for a two-bedroom up to the low $400,000 for a three-bedroom.

Upper Greenville is generally considered north of Mockingbird. There is a little section of Upper Greenville, which is east of Greenville Ave., South of Lovers Lane, north of the Katy Trail, west of Skillman. Most people know this area as where Central Market is located. It is plush with restaurants, grocery stores, transportation, parks, trails and health and wellness. The condominiums in this section range anywhere from $150k for a 2BR up to $375K for a 2BR. I would generally say this might be one of the best lesser known areas in Dallas for affordable living and walkability, and general local of living. It is also in Stonewall Jackson Elementary School's district, which is a top-rated elementary school in Dallas ISD.

Lake Highlands is an area known for its several subdivisions within certain elementary school areas that are in Richardson Independent School District, City of Dallas. Because of the Richardson ISD designation this is a desirable location for families due to location to downtown and the school ratings being so good. The condominiums in this area range in the $60,000 up to mid $200,000 range at the Copperfield Condominiums. The reason for the low prices is that most of these condominiums are non-warrantable which means there are too many investor owned properties as compared to owners living the condo homes.

Far North Dallas/Addison

This area generally has strong economic and social ties to the City of Addison, Farmers Branch, Richardson, Carrollton and Plano. Far North Dallas is generally known as the area north of I-635 and west of Coit and South of President George Bush Turnpike and east of the Dallas North Tollway. The city of Addison is west of the Dallas North Tollway with a west border of Marsh lane up to President George Bush Turnpike and south to roughly Arapaho.

The Far North Dallas area is home to the Galleria Mall has almost 2 million sq. ft. of retail space containing over 200 stores and serves as a central shopping hub in Dallas.

This North Dallas area is also well known for its private schools Greenhill, Parish Episcopal, and is also home to some of the best elementary schools such as Brentfield, Mohawk, Canyon Creek, and Prestonwood which are a part of the Richardson Independent School district that feeds into JJ Pearce High School and Richardson High School.

This Far North Dallas area is popular area and buyers are going to great lengths to bring the area values up tremendously by updating homes. Home values have also been boosted by supply and demand. The condominium, townhome, garden homes are some of the best values to buy in the North Dallas area. Some of these new developments have brought an enthusiastic energy to these areas. The price points in the Far North Dallas area range from the low $80,000 for a small one-bedroom up to mid million-dollar range for new home Garden Homes at the Lawn at Glen Abbey. The Bonaventure Condo is a high-rise Condominium in the Far North Dallas area. It has an outdoor walking track with outdoor pool, two onsite secured access tennis courts, complete indoor fitness center, saunas, hot tubs and swimming pools, lakeside with lush gardens. Prices for these condominiums range from the low $300,000 with 1,685 square feet up to high $700,000 price range with close to 4,000 square feet. There are also new townhomes built in this area at University Place in the mid $350,000 range for almost 2,000 square feet and a small yard.

The city of Addison is known for its night life, restaurants, and social scene. The prices in Addison for Condominiums, Townhomes, and Garden homes range anywhere from the low $300,000 up to the $500,000 range for Garden Homes.

Northwest Dallas

Northwest Dallas is the corridor stretching from Love Field airport going up the Stemmons Freeway Corridor with the Asian Trade District on the far northwest edge of the community. This area has not been as developed as others, but recently has taken on a major change in scenery and buyers have gone to great lengths to bring this neighborhood back to life by refurbishing houses and because of this many of these homes have become quite valuable. Like much of Dallas the proximity to major thoroughfares, hospitals, entertainment, and city centers has increased lot values tremendously in recent years. There are several condominium and townhome complexes in this area highlighted by the Pierremont townhome community which is on the North side of Northwest Highway, halfway in between Midway and Marsh. This complex was built in 1981 and has a clubhouse, community pool, and it is gated. Rosser Park is farther north just south of I-635. Amenities in this village include a beautifully landscaped pool area, tennis courts, and clubhouse.

Surrounding Dallas

Condo living is not limited to downtown, uptown, Oak Lawn, and North Dallas. In Dallas Suburban communities, consumers are demanding a better quality of life, better management of the environment, and a maintenance free life-style. These are all best available through condominium living. As a result, self-supporting urban villages with high-rise condominiums, condominiums, Townhomes, and Garden Homes are popping up all around the city of Dallas. These consumers want convenience and are choosing to live where they can have it all.

Having it all means convenient shopping, entertainment, schools, and medical services. This community is also concerned with preserving the environmental quality of air and water through proper application of conservation and civil engineering practices. Newer green friendly communities emphasize places where children can play safely, bike trails that connect to larger trails, clean waterways that run through parks, and places where people feel like they are playing in nature. The suburbs have plenty of room to meet these needs and will capitalize on green-friendly neighborhoods as a place to work, live, and play.

The Dallas North Tollway connects Frisco to Downtown Dallas. The Central Expressway that connects residents from Richardson, Plano, Allen, and McKinney to downtown Dallas has made these commutes bearable. The Dart Train goes as far north as Plano, and there are plans to extend it farther North past McKinney. There is Dart Train that now goes up the Interstate 35 corridor to Denton. These areas are all exciting, entertaining, full service communities.

There are several townhome, garden home and condominium communities springing up in these suburban areas. At the writing of this in July of 2018 there are currently over 15 new condominium, townhome, Garden home developments in Frisco and Plano. Price points range from low $300,000 up to mid $800,000 for Garden Homes at Wyndsor Pointe in Frisco. A new high-rise development is the Windrose Tower in Plano at the new $3 billion Legacy West development. This is the first of its kind in the Frisco and Plano area. People want a simple life style that is more turn key and ready for them to travel, go to work, enjoy their families and friends. This new life style based on the belief that we do create the world we live in is focusing on a more sustainable environment in which we are conscious of our surroundings, we cooperate with all living beings, in this process we take up less space even in these suburban settings. For all of these new condominium, townhome, and garden home developments please go to www.CondoLivingDallas.com for all the latest prices and new inventory.

Chapter 2 — Condominiums Defined

Condominiums in Brief

You don't have own land and build a house to own real estate. You can purchase an individual unit in a large building and still have the advantages of real estate ownership and more.

This style of living is popular because it's mostly maintenance free. That's right — no more cutting grass, spraying weeds, trimming hedges, repairing a needy house, pool maintenance, or a million other tasks. If you are like me you would rather spend your time, especially free time, doing things you really love rather than work around the house. Yet this benefit only scratches the surface of why this fabulous way of living is attractive to so many people just like you.

> "The fellow that owns his own home is always
> just coming out of the hardware store."
> *-Kin Hubbard, American humorist*

This association style of living can be found throughout Dallas and the surrounding communities (each condo, townhome, garden home, can be like its own little city). This can be found anywhere from downtown Dallas as far north as Frisco, McKinney and Denton and South into Mansfield and west to Fort Worth and east to Rockwall.

People who buy into the condo lifestyle tell me they enjoy living the turn key lifestyle. This is a style that gives them choices and freedoms they never thought were possible. Most people who adopt this condo style living wish they would have made the jump sooner. Most people feel that if they buy a condominium it will lose its value and leave their investment worthless. This could not be farther from the truth and often times condominiums and townhomes have great values and better values than single family homes.

This sky is falling fear of the condominium market generally comes from a lack of information. We are often times in the real estate industry drowning in information and starving for wisdom.

> "Any purchase is better than renting, and owning a condo is a great investment for many reasons! If those reasons include wanting to have more time and money, then buying is the choice!
>
> *-Dr. Hank Seitz, Agent Wealth Network*

Comparatively speaking, if a developer builds a subdivision in the North Dallas suburbs it takes 4-8 years depending on the size to sell the complex. Why would a condominium market be different? In Dallas the Luxury High End market condominiums take 4-8 years to sell. This is a result of the price point, not that the sky is falling. Any difficulties in the condominium market are due to a slow economy, price point, in which all real estate investments are affected equally.

Of course, factors such as poor planning by the developer and/or the under capitalization of the project can impact a particular development. In Chapter 5, I will give questions to ask that will help you get to know the developer.

As for concerns about downsizing, leaving a lifestyle that has been the norm for decades is a tremendous challenge for most people. But not challenging your comfort level is generally what keeps you from moving to levels of living that you never thought possible.

> "Growing means you're leaving the comfort zone.
>
> *-Brian Buffini*

Ask those who have made the leap and they will tell you it was not easy, but the rewards have been far better than anticipated. Better yet, listen to the testimonies at www.CondoLivingDallas.com.

What exactly is a condominium?

A condominium is legally considered a form of real estate ownership. The three most common forms of real estate ownership are fee simple (owning land and a home), condominium (owning a unit within a building), and cooperative (buying shares of a property).

In modern property law, a condominium is the individual ownership of one dwelling unit and the legally described airspace within that unit, with an undivided ownership interest in the land and other components of the building shared in common with other owners of dwelling units in the building.

Garden Home/Zero Lot Line, Single Family Attached (SFA), Duplexes often times do have a mandatory membership in a homeowner's association. For the sake of simplicity in this book the term condominium will refer to all of these types of homes unless otherwise stated.

The terms "Garden Home", "Single Family Attached", "High-Rise", "Duplex" and "Townhome" describe architecturally what a residence looks like. A high-rise condominium is a unit within a multi-level building. A townhome condominium and Single Family Attached are a house with an adjoining wall to another townhome or Single Family Attached. A Garden Home is a standalone house.

> "By using vertical space more effectively, you not only make more room for greenery but shorter commutes also mean less pressure on CO_2 emission problems and by freeing up time

> now spent on unproductive commuter trains,
> people would have more options in their lives."
> *-Minoru Mori, Japanese Real Estate Tycoon*

When you buy a condominium, you receive a deed for your specific space just like you would for a house. Basically, you own everything between the walls of your unit.

In high-rises, townhomes and condominiums, you also own a proportionate share of the common elements of the land and buildings (assuming the land is owned by the association rather than leased). This includes hallways, elevators, pools, fitness centers, and other public areas common to the building. It is an undivided interest, meaning your rights in the common area are shared with other owners. There are exceptions, and these are usually spelled out in the condominium documents.

Put simply, if it's inside your unit you own it and it's your responsibility. For example, if your refrigerator breaks it is up to you to fix it, not the building management. On the other hand, if the elevator is not working, it's up to the building management to have it repaired.

As a condominium owner, you are governed by state laws as well as specific rules and regulations set in your condominium documents. We will discuss this in greater detail in the next chapter.

What is a High-Rise Condominium?

When people say "condominium", what comes to mind most often is a high-rise condominium. If you own a high-rise condominium, you own a unit within a multi-story building and share an undivided interest in common areas such as hallways, fitness centers, pools, roof top decks, community centers. High-Rise condominiums can be newly constructed or renovated older buildings. Unit sizes range from lofts to 7,000+ square foot penthouse spaces.

This style of property is often popular for the added luxurious amenities, such as 24 hours/7days concierge service, Spas, 24hours/7days food service and Private garages. While high-rises are synonymous with downtown areas, some high-rise condominium are found in other areas of the city.

Pros

- High Rise condominiums are normally positioned in denser urban neighborhoods and are more than likely to have all of life's necessities within walking distance.

- No more maintaining the yard, painting the exterior, cleaning the gutters, repairing the roof, or cleaning the pool. The association will hire someone to take care of all the outside tasks and possibly a few inside depending on the association. In a well-run association someone else will keep your place maintained and looking good regardless of whether you're home or on vacation.

- Not everyone can offer amenities like swimming pools, tennis courts, fitness centers, concierge services, roof top decks, etc....By buying into an association for a reasonable fee, you can enjoy the luxuries you may not have been able to afford as a traditional home owner- and someone else will do the maintenance.

- Rules and regulations are laid out for all to follow. Knowing what your neighbor will and will not be allowed to do provides a sense of security. These rules and regulations protect you and your investment. The best part is you don't have to enforce the rules. This is done by the association board.

- Best of all you get to do this and still build equity!

Cons

- You have neighbors who also share a common interest and rights equal to yours.

- You must obey the outlined rules and regulations and you will be held accountable by the association. In a sense, you lose some control by having an association determine what is acceptable, but most associations function very well and mirror rules and regulations regarding quiet enjoyment that city laws have already addressed.

- You may end up paying for luxuries you never use, such as pools, concierge, valet, etc....That is not all bad because having those also brings value to your unit if you decide to resell at a later time.

What is a Hotel Condominium?

These are typically found in major cities or resort towns such as Chicago, New York City, Aspen, Miami, Southern Florida, and California. This added innovation to the condominium market was started in the early 1980's in Southern Florida Miami area as condo conversions. It can be an investment for people who wish to purchase real estate as an investment for income and appreciation, rather than a residence.

Purchasing a hotel condominium is similar to a regular condominium because it comes with a deed, association documents, and will have a board of directors. The building will be just like a hotel and likely have a successful five-star hotel managing the property. The only extra documentation you will receive is the one that explains the relationship between the hotel operation and the owners. It is imperative to understand the contracts that have been established between the hotel operators and the developers of the condominium.

Many costs are divided between the hotel and owners, such as upkeep, administration costs, maid service, furniture, linens, and more. Each hotel condominium operation will have numerous variations regarding shared costs and how profit is divided. The operating documents will explain in detail how this relationship will be managed.

Living and leasing arrangements will vary from project to project. In order to use your condominium yourself, you may need to make a reservation and pay like anyone else-especially if you will use hotel services while living there.

The hotel may give you the option to lease it out yourself. Because the hotel needs to make an income, it will likely have some restraints on leasing, especially during peak money-making times of the year. There are many options regarding the arrangements set up in hotel condominium documents, so investigate thoroughly to ensure the opportunity fits your needs before making an investment.

Townhomes/Townhome Condominiums

There is distinction between townhomes and townhome condominiums in Texas. A townhome comes with survey, so the owner actually owns the land on which the townhome is located within the survey boundaries. Townhome condominiums do not have a survey, so they are traditional condominiums. Whether or not a townhome or townhome condominium was zoned as a townhome with a survey or townhome without a survey is up to the original developer. A survey outlines the specific lot for a townhome, a townhome will have shared wall or walls and the association documents outline how this works.

Townhome/Townhome Condominiums are often found in suburbs because they require more land per unit than an urban condominium or high rise. In urban settings, such as downtown areas they tend to be more vertical with several flights of stairs up to even a 4th story roof top deck. Having multiple floors is a good thing for those who want space for working, hobbies, or just time alone.

Pros

- There is more autonomy living in a townhome compared to a high-rise or condominium because you do not have to be bothered by neighbors above or below you or as you go from townhome to car. Even though a townhome is attached to other units they still feel more like a house than an apartment.

- Townhomes usually have more than one level, private garages, and larger private patios, decks or small yard as opposed to the balconies or small fences found in many high-rise condominiums.

- As discussed earlier, being a part of an association allows the individual owner an undivided ownership in amenities like swimming pools, tennis courts, etc....which might not otherwise be affordable to the average home owner.

- Townhomes are usually less expensive per square foot than a high rise or condominiums (unless they are located in a downtown, or near downtown location).

- Like a condominium, the owner does not have to worry about lawn care, common areas, and exterior maintenance issues.

Cons

- Depending on how well your common wall is insulated, you may find your neighbors' noise quite bothersome. This is less of a problem in newer buildings, which have to adhere to new building codes pertaining to joining walls. Some of the older condominiums have added insulation to these walls to work the problems, but it is always worth investigating.

Garden Home/Zero Lot Line

Garden/Zero Lot line homes differ the most from high rise, townhome condominiums, and standard condominiums because they are simply private standalone homes with association dues that cover mainly lawn and common areas. Association fees are usually cheaper than condominium dues because there is very little common area. However, as noted in Chapter One many of these communities that are gated have common areas that may include a neighborhood playground, walking paths, tennis courts, clubhouses, pools, and much, much more.

Pros

- Many of these communities are gated with luxurious amenities like Tennis Courts, Parks, Walking Paths, Clubhouses, etc....

- Garden Homes generally do have a small yard. If an owner has a green thumb, they can have the opportunity to garden and mow a little lawn if they choose.

- Because there is land associated with the home there is a survey, so the owner does own the land and the home on the lot.

- No attached walls.

Cons

- Associations do not cover as many items for the house in the Garden Home communities.

- Generally larger with more square feet in the Garden Homes so there is more maintenance and items to take care. Fewer turnkeys.

Single Family Attached/Duplex

Single Family Attached and Duplexes are becoming more and more common in urban settings. Where these are often different than the previous mentioned condominiums and Garden style homes is there is no HOA. However, as the name states it is attached to another home like a townhome. So, the SFA's have a survey, they are attached to another home, with most of the time no HOA. A duplex is similar to a SFA in that it has attached walls. Sometimes the Duplex is sold as a single unit with both units together or sold individually with each side of the duplex being its own separate unit. A SFA if an individual was to buy both sides of the SFA could technically be a duplex.

Pros

- Homes have surveys, so the land and home's space are owned 100% by the owner.

- Smaller yards.

Cons

- Owners have an attached wall similar to townhomes.

- Generally, do not have Home Owners Associations so the upkeep is the responsibility of the home owner.

Condominiums Are for Everyone

Baby Boomers

Many baby boomers that are empty nesters are looking for a maintenance free lifestyle. They didn't experience the great depression or WWII, so letting go of the old life for a new one comes more naturally. They have spent most of their lives in suburbia and are more than ready to sell off their lawn mowers, yard rakes, garden tools, weed whackers, and all other sorts of expensive (and often back breaking) equipment.

That means they are leaving behind long days of repairing decks, water heaters, painting, roofs, fences, to finally do what they have always wanted to do. Condominium living gives them an opportunity to lock the door and leave whenever they want, without warning about maintenance. They have more time with grandkids, take more vacations, join volunteer organizations, start new hobbies, write books, exercise, go to movies, go to a show, sporting events, or just relax and read a book. It's almost like being on vacation in your own home.

Divorcees and Widows/Widowers
This group is looking for condominium style living. For single parents with kids, the low maintenance lifestyle of a townhome, garden home, or SFA, with a yard for kids to play in may be more appealing than a high-rise condominium. For other families with kids, the security of a high-rise condominium in an area that has playgrounds and parks may be more important.

Retirees
Retirees benefit from condo living because they are often looking to downsize and simplify their lifestyle, so they can travel, visit family, and socialize. They enjoy living maintenance free in close proximity to medical facilities, theatres, upscale shops, art galleries, museums, parks and restaurants. This type of investment also allows retirees to better manage their estates.

Think about it. Many retirees live in houses full of treasures they have collected over the years and stuffed away in attics, closets, basements, garages, and storage sheds. Most will tell you that their stuff starts to own them.

To move into a condominium, you do need to get rid of a majority of your stuff. Those who have done it will tell you the experience is absolutely liberating. Unencumbered by the upkeep of a large home, these residents have the time and freedom to start new hobbies, visit friends, join card clubs, walk in a park, take trips, start a Qigong class, spend time with the grand kids, write a book, or join a gym.

Another big benefit is when retirees do pass on, their kids are not left with a big mess to clean up. Anyone and eventually everyone who loses their parents knows how much work it takes to clean up a house that has years of knick knacks and mementos. This can be quite a stressful undertaking for siblings who already who already have family responsibilities of their own, especially if they live out of town and sibling relationships are put to the test. So, in addition to all the freedom that comes with downsizing, retirees can take responsibility for their own estates. What a great gift to leave your children.

After buying condominiums, some retirees completely start over by getting rid of everything except their cars. They have the time of their lives buying new furniture, cookware, clothes...you name it. How many chances like that do people get?

Indeed, these are not your traditional break-out the slippers and watch TV retirees of yesteryear. They have discovered their second wind and are reinventing the American Dream. Don't even think about putting this generation in a retirement home, they are setting a pace for generations to follow. They are living examples of the phrase Colonel Sanders used in his later, most successful years: *"You will rust out before you wear out, so keep moving."*

Generation X
Generation X grew up in the suburbs during the cold war. They are very entrepreneurial, and this generation saw their home values plummet and their homes taken from them in many cases by the Great Recession from 2008-2013. This also represents one of the largest pools of real estate investors.

This generation is open to living the Condominium lifestyle and has been on the forefront of the development of the condominium life style. The condominium market is prime for this generation. As part of this generation and living in a condominium, I can attest that it suits a simple life style that can include all the luxuries of life.

Millenials

Oh boy Millennials might be the most talked about generation since the baby boomers. Funny the Millennials are their off spring. This generation is career oriented and waiting longer to start a family. A record number of people in this generation are staying single. But single or married, the idea of living, working, and playing all within a few city blocks is tremendously exciting.

This group was predominantly raised in the suburbs and is tired of strip malls and being stuck in out of the way suburbia. Urban condominium living is where they thrive because they are close to everything. Quality nights and weekends matter as much as workdays to the millennial.

Generation Z

Generation Z is also known as the iGeneration. This generation has grown up with an iPhone, computer, iPad, or some other computer gadget since they were born. This generation teaches their parents how to use these items.

This group will be interested in a style of living that will bring about more of what they know and like. Their generation of condominiums will be digital friendly. When buying a condominium, they will be more likely concerned about the way the information flows than whether they get a fireplace. They need room for the big screen TVs and the ability to have the world at their fingertips through digital media.

For any of these groups, a low maintenance lifestyle means more time to spend on what's important. With how busy most people are today, that's more important than ever.

By now you are beginning to appreciate and understand the many benefits of condominium living. For many people it's the best possible lifestyle choice.

If you think condominium living is right for you and you're ready to take the next step, the next chapters offer specifics that will guide you into this amazing form of ownership. As you will see, a little common sense paired with the right information is all you will need. To find out more about condominiums please go to our website at www.CondoLivingDallas.com.

Chapter 3 — How is a Condominium Developed?

Let's say Joe Developer starts a company called Builders Incorporated with the purpose of building condominiums. Before he may sell any of the newly built condominium units, he must first declare to the local governing agency that he's building with the intent of creating a condominium community. The document required for this is the Declaration. This document also declares that an Association will be responsible for total operation of the condominium community, using rules and guidelines stated within the declaration.

This association is usually created as a nonprofit corporation and consists of all the owners of the condominium units in the development. Until enough units are sold, the association includes only the developer. In order to create a legal corporation, Articles of Incorporation are created stating the corporation's purpose. This is filed with the Secretary of State.

This newly formed corporation needs a Board of Directors. This governing body is responsible for administration of the association and is elected by the owners of the condominiums in the development. By-Laws are then created. These govern how the board operates administratively and operationally. By-laws create the procedure for giving the board of directors the power and guidance to make decisions on behalf of and in the best interest of all the association's members.

> "Every person who invests in well-selected real estate in a growing section of a prosperous community adopts the surest and safest method of becoming independent, for real estate is the basis of wealth."
>
> *-Theodore Roosevelt, 26th U.S. President*

Even though we now have a declaration, articles of incorporation, and by-Laws as governing documents, a fourth document is usually added. A Rules and Regulations document further clarifies items that may be unclear or not covered in the declaration, articles of incorporation, and by-laws.

This may oversimplify the process of creating a functioning condominium, but it is imperative for potential owners to understand these basics first. Your realtor can obtain these documents for you to review. Below is a more detailed explanation of each document.

Governing Documents

The order of authority for governing condominium documents are as follows:

> Condominium Act Before January 1st, 1994
> Uniform Condominium Act After January 1994
> Declaration
> Articles of Incorporation
> Bylaws
> Rules & Regulations
> Condominiums created before adoption
> Uniform Condominium Act After January 1st, 1994

Declaration

The declaration is the first document that you should become familiar with before purchasing a condominium. It declares what type of legal entity the property is going to be. This document is recorded with the county to define for the public the developer's plan for the project and actually brings the condominium into existence when it is filed with the county register of deeds office.

This document is prepared by the developer and must comply with the requirements of the Uniform Condominium Act.

In addition, the declaration defines which portions of the development will be owned by the owners and which will be owned by the association. It creates the boundaries of each unit and the common areas. The declaration creates the framework for the operation and management of the association, with details about restrictions, covenants, and rules designed to promote an amicable living environment.

It also defines the relationship between the developer and owners as to how the transition from developer to owner will take place.

The first part of the declaration gives the legal name of the condominium and the date the condominium property regime was made and by whom, meaning the developer's corporation or LLC, and where the developer is from.

Articles

The declaration consists of many sections called articles. These include the following:

Definitions – Gives the meanings of terminology used in the declaration.

Condominium Units – Provides the number of residential and/or commercial units, vertical and horizontal dimensions, construction materials, number of buildings, systems and equipment in units. If this is a phased project, the declaration will state the number of units in each phase.

Common Elements – Defines the common elements, such as a fitness center, swimming pool, lawns, roofs, and community room. These common elements are all portions of the condominium other than the units. The association does not own the common elements or areas. They are jointly owned by the people who have purchased their property and have joined the association. Ownership of the common elements shall be defined by a percentage of each unit and will go with that unit if it is sold.

Limited Common Elements – Defines a portion of the common elements allocated for the exclusive us of one or more, but fewer than all, of the units. For example, a fitness center — although a common area — is limited to resident use only and is not for commercial purposes.

Easements – Explains the types of easements, such as utilities. This allows utility providers the right to install, repair, and maintain services as needed for the operation of a residential community. The developer usually will have a blanket easement in his favor for the ingress and egress of his contractors or employees for the purpose of improvements, restoration, or construction of additional property.

Architectural and operational control committees – Defines the responsibility of committees for governing the residential units and related limited common elements. These committees oversee any physical changes made to any part of the building, including the units. Always check with this committee before doing anything -- from painting your front door to remodeling the inside of your condominium. This also includes satellite dishes as they affect the appearance of the building. The main goal of this committee is to protect the integrity and value of the condominium by establishing and enforcing reasonable rules and regulations.

Restrictions – Describes any limits on the type and amount of business you may operate from your unit. Typically, units are restricted to single family residential use. In addition, this article defines the rules for pets, use of property, antennas, vehicle parking, signs, security, unsightly appearances, acts affecting insurance, trash containers and collection, equipment, leasing of units, nuisances and offensive activity, and the procedure for enforcement.

Maintenance – Describes maintenance responsibilities for both the owner and association. This section is helpful in determining what you the owner are responsible for repairing and/or replacing, and what the association is responsible for. Generally, snow removal and lawn maintenance are the association's biggest expenses.

Association – Identifies the association's legal name, who is included in the membership, and the initial members of the board of directors. Remember that even though the association is identified by the declaration, it is not created by the declaration. The association is a corporate entity, usually a nonprofit corporation, and must actually be created by filing Articles of Incorporation with the Secretary of State in order to be in existence.

Insurance – Defines the authority to purchase casualty, property, director and officers' liability, and general liability insurances. It will also cover minimum amounts for each type of coverage.

Rights Reserved to Developer – Gives the developer the right to place on common areas sales offices, fencing, construction equipment, advertising signs, banners, and other promotional facilities needed to successfully sell or lease units. This article also gives the developer rights to do business and sign contracts on behalf of the association without the association's approval. When the association is transferred over to the unit owners, the association at that time will have the option to renegotiate or terminate any of these contracts. Read this section thoroughly as it tells you ahead of time the developer's rights over the owners. This assumes the project is new and the project is not finished, or that new phases will follow.

Amendment of Declaration – Describes the procedure and minimal participation required from the owners to change any part of the declaration. Most of the time this article protects the association from impulsive changes or emotional surges that make sense at the time, but later prove to be detrimental to the whole.

Most declarations will at a minimum contain the above information. The declaration does not have to be approved by any government regulatory authority. However, it does have to be prepared in compliance with the requirements of the Texas Condominium Act.

Articles of Incorporation

In order to incorporate the association, it is necessary to have the Articles of Incorporation filled out by an attorney familiar with the Texas Nonprofit Corporation Act. These articles of incorporation, once filed with the Secretary of State, will provide the unit owners who make up the association a wall of corporate protection. It also usually identifies the original board of directors and defines the general purpose and powers of the corporation.

By-Laws

The by-laws can be a part of the declaration or a separate document altogether. These are prepared in compliance with the Texas Nonprofit Corporation Act. By-laws are the road map that tells the board of directors how to conduct their board meetings. You will save yourself much frustration if you take the time to understand the by-laws.

A simple list of duties for board members, which are explained in the bylaws, is as follows:

- Adopt and publish rules
- Enforce the provisions of the declaration, by-laws, and rules
- Employ a manager, maintenance personnel, or outside contractors
- Prepare and adopt an annual budget
- Provide for the maintenance and care of common areas
- Collect assessments
- Manage any contracts for maintenance, repairs, or improvements
- Carry sufficient insurance on common areas and pay premiums
- Maintain a ledger of receipt and expenditures
- Produce financial statements
- Appoint committees for specific tasks and lengths of time

You will also find a job description for each officer and the rules that govern them in the by-laws, as well as descriptions on how committees work and who they are responsible to, the amount and type of insurance required for the property, the maximum amount of money the board of directors can spend on unexpected expenses or improvements without approval from owners, frequency of meetings, attendance at meetings, what requires unit owner votes, and election procedures.

HINT: *Once you select a particular condominium, I strongly recommend you ask for copies of meeting minutes to see what issues have been discussed for the last six months.*

Rules and Regulations
These documents complement the declaration by giving more definitions of rules and Regulations

Associations Defined

The terms "condominium" and "association" are completely different concepts. As stated earlier, a condominium is a form of ownership of a piece of real estate in which the owner acquires title to a property and ownership of common areas with other owners in the same complex.

An association typically refers to a homeowner's association, which is composed of all of the owners in a particular development.

An association can exist with respect to a typical single-family home subdivision or in a condominium owner situation.

Financial Documents

You should preview several financial documents to see how financially sound the association is. If you are looking at a new condominium development, there won't be any historical data to provide clues. In this case, my suggestion is to ask for the proposed budgets and make sure they contain at a minimum the line items on page 43.

HINT: If this is the developer's first condominium project, you need to be especially careful and have a professional look at the budget numbers. I recommend having an attorney who specializes in condominiums to assist you. For attorneys that I endorse please go to http://www.CondoLivingDallas.com.

If this is not the developer's first condominium project, I recommend getting in touch with the association from previous projects. Most associations are more than happy to help. Either they are eager to brag about their community or complain about the mess the developer left them. More often than not, you will find good, healthy relationships between developers and associations because developers want happy residents who will tell their friends how satisfied they are.

If you are looking at a condominium development that has a fully established association with some history behind it, then you should at minimum get the following financial information:

- Statement of budget amounts versus actual expenses
- Copy of the current month's balance sheet
- Copy of the current month's profit and loss statement
- Copy of the independent CPA audit for the last fiscal year
- Percentage of the owners' assessments that are put into a reserve fund
- Current balance in the reserve fund
- Copy of the last reserve study
- Evidence that the fund is being replaced as per the reserve study
- Name of the institution that holds the association's fund along with investment strategy

Association Fees

When you own a condominium, you also pay a monthly assessment. This is a unit owner's proportionate share of common expenses. The type of condominium you live in determines the common area expenses you are responsible for. For example, high-rise condominiums usually have a nice lobby, elevators, and hallways to maintain. A townhome condominium, on the other hand, usually will not have any of these. Some of the basic common expenses that all condominium associations are responsible for are snow removal, landscaping, insurance, water, reserve fund, and common area electrical or gas. Below are typical budget items for a high-rise condominium:

- Administration
- Management fees
- Legal
- Accounting
- Office expenses
- Association and board meeting supplies

- Holiday decorations
- Supplies for fitness center and community room
- Labor Costs
- Manager
- Live-in caretaker
- Concierge
- Utilities
- Water and sewer
- Electricity common areas
- Gas
- Trash removal
- Cable
- Telephone/Whatever Whenever Service
- Service Contracts
- HVAC services
- Mechanical inspections
- Fire sprinkler inspections
- Alarms inspection
- Garage doors, heating/air
- Insurance Property Liability
- Umbrella
- Crime
- Director and officer coverage
- Landscape
- Grounds contract
- Exterior sprinkler maintenance
- Snow removal
- Repairs
- General Maintenance
- Cleaning contract
- Window washing
- General repairs
- Supplies
- Labor
- Miscellaneous
- Five Percent Contingency Fund
- Reserve Fund

HINT: *As a realtor, I always insist that buyers have a contingency in the purchase contract allowing time for an attorney review of all documents before closing. This way, as a potential buyer, you can get out of the purchase contract and have your earnest deposit refunded if you find something in the documents that is disagreeable to you.*

Your Personal Involvement

When buying into a condominium, you decide how involved you want to be. If you plan on volunteering to be on the board or any committees, your workload can be tremendous as this is a big commitment. You will spend a lot of time working on behalf of the entire community. Unity depends on members putting personal ambitions aside for the good of the whole.

If you are not planning on serving on the board or any committees, then your participation may be as minimal as attending association meetings that are normally held annually. It is not uncommon for the association to hire a management company to oversee day-to-day operations. Some condominiums don't hire management companies and therefore may rely more on volunteers. This can be a tremendous savings and thus reduces monthly association fees. However, this is not normally the case and will be spelled out in the declaration.

Improvements to Your Condominium

If you are planning on buying a condominium with the idea of making a few changes to any part of the building that affects the exterior appearance in any way -- including your entryway, balcony, or parking spot --it's always a good idea to talk to the board first.

Some common things that require board approval are satellite dishes, decorations, flower beds, and squirrel or bird feeders. It is the board's responsibility to see that nothing negatively affects the value of the property.

Pet Policies

Many condominium residents have pets. Rules regarding pets run the gamut. If the condominium association has been around for a while, the pet policy may have been changed a few times. You can find this information not only in the declaration, but also in any amendments that have been made.

Work/Play

If you are planning on running a business out of your condominium, check for restrictions. Having a garage sale, yard sale, or rummage sale may be prohibited in your association. Also, patios and balconies may have restrictions regarding weight and specific items allowed.

Sometimes the rules on this issue will reflect the city's rules. All of this is covered in the declaration or the rules and regulations.

Security

Security is always a concern and most condominiums have state-of-the-art security systems to monitor who comes into the building and parking areas. Some condos have 24-hour manned security service. If you are considering a security system on your specific unit that is not addressed in the declaration, then you will need to contact the board.

Maintenance

Maintenance on the exterior of your unit can vary from place to place. In a townhome condominium, you may be responsible for such things as the siding and roof. This will be spelled out in the Declaration. Make sure you're very clear on what you're responsible for, otherwise you could end up with some very high unexpected expenses.

If you have questions regarding the buying or selling process, please contact us at info@CondoLivingDallas.com or 214-552-9304.

Chapter 4 — The First Steps

The Smart Buyer's Mindset

Before buying your high-rise condominium, townhome, condominium, or zero lot line, you need to concentrate on the type of information that will allow you to make a logical rather than emotional decision.

The reason many buyers err on the emotional side is that emotions feel a lot better than logic. But an emotional decision almost always leads to a major cause of buyers' remorse.

Every human is vulnerable, at least to some degree, to the exhilarating but blinding experience of buying on excitement. You might feel like you have to snatch up this great deal now before someone else gets it.

You're better off letting the emotional dust settle before signing on the dotted line. Channel your excitement in another direction, one that ignores the obvious allure, by putting your enthusiasm and energy into getting answers to the right questions.

> "We shape our dwellings, and afterwards our dwellings shape us."
> -Winston Churchill, British Prime Minister

The Realtor Advantage

One of the biggest complaints I hear from owners is, "I wish someone would have told me that before I bought." They will, if you ask. Many buyers do not know what the right questions to ask are when it comes to the Dallas condominium market. Besides knowing what to ask, you should know whom to ask because this information comes from a variety of sources.

The first person you should talk to is a Realtor who specializes in condominium sales. A condominium specialist can tell you things that a developer won't and will have the connections needed to get reliable answers to your questions.

I have found that numerous condominium projects in Dallas have secrets. Maybe a condominium lacks sufficient sound barrier between units. Maybe traffic at certain times of the day is unreasonable. Maybe it's taking an unreasonable amount of time to complete a punch list of items that need to be fixed on a new project. Maybe the number of rentals will negatively affect the long-term market value. Maybe there is suspicious handling of association funds. The list could go on ad infinitum.

A specialist also knows to ask less obvious questions. Has the developer been fiscally responsible in other projects? Will new developments in the area block views? Is the project overpriced? Is the association under-funded? The list goes on. That is why it is important to work with someone who is experienced in the market and can guide you through the process. As a condominium specialist this is what I do.

Use the questions in Chapter 5 to get the answers you need from the developer and association before determining if a particular condominium is a good safe investment for you. Before you do that, lets narrow the search by determining three things: location, buying power, and style of condominium.

Location, Location, Location
The real estate phrase "location, location, location" remains the key factor when deciding where to buy. Although it

seems this sage advice has been around forever, I believe it needs explanation to be put into perspective.

Location means something different to everyone. A location could be the west coast, east coast, Dallas, or Iowa, it could mean 5678 Main Street #231...More importantly, location concerns the surrounding area of a particular address and the services that are provided. Examples of relevant factors are proximity to good schools, transportation, recreational facilities, shopping and commercial centers, entertainment, medical facilities, places of worship, and availability of parking.

HINT: *Sometimes it is easier to narrow down where you do not to live, then work with what is left. Buying a home is a process of elimination, not a selection process. To narrow down what's available in a particular area go to www.CondoLivingDallas.com. Here you will find a list of all the condominiums, townhomes, and zero lot lines for sale in Dallas and the surrounding areas.*

An excellent way to learn about an area is to talk to residents who live there. The don't have to live in the same building or on the same block. They do have to share the geographic area that provides products and services to that same community. All urban and suburban areas have gathering points - coffee shops, restaurants, and places of worship where you can strike up conversations.

Keep in mind that one person's opinion can be totally different from the neighbor who lives right next door. Human experiences vary with personality and are not always reliable. If you talk to enough people, you will have a better chance of getting a good feel for the demographics, crime rate, and economic development of an area.

HINT: *Other ways of getting information include checking with public services such as the police department and the city's economic development manager. You can also surf demographics web sites. These links can be found at www.CondoLivingDallas.com.*

Buying Power with Loan Pre-Approval

If you are serious about purchasing a condominium, one of the most important things you can do is get pre-approved for a loan. This determines your buying power and is not a commitment on your part. Instead, a pre-approval is only an offer from the bank of how much they are willing to lend based on the accuracy of the information provided.

Some resellers won't even let you into their unit unless you are pre-approved because of all the hard work required to prepare a home for sale and security issues. Also, many people in condominiums work from home and would have to leave their home/work for a couple of hours while the property is being shown. This is an inconvenience they are willing to bear for serious buyers, but if you are just window shopping, they understandably would rather not have the interruption.

If you have sold your home before, you understand the amount of work it takes to prepare the house for sale. You've also felt the hope and excitement of having a potential buyer. When sellers open their homes for showing, only to be let down by the perspective buyers who are just looking for design ideas or won't be serious for another year, they learn to draw the line at pre-approvals only.

"If I were asked to name the chief benefit of
the house, I should say: the house shelters
day dreaming, the house protects the dream-
er, the house allows one to dream in peace."
    -*Gaston Bachelard, French scientist/philosopher*

Being pre-approved also gives you power when negotiating a price because you are a pre-qualified buyer. With the ups and downs of the mortgage industry, being pre-approved lets the seller know that your deal has a good chance of going through. Sellers will take your offer seriously and eagerly participate in negotiations.

Signing a contract with a prospective buyer takes the home off the market, making it unavailable to the public. That means a sale is pending and any potential buyers will assume the property is sold. What seller wants to tie up a property in a contract unless the buyer is pre-approved?

Getting pre-approved early also allows you to correct any errors on your credit report. You may think your record is clean, only to be extremely disappointed and frustrated when the bank denies your loan because of a $225 outstanding bill from five years ago you didn't even know existed.

With this pre-approval you know exactly what your buying power is. That saves you time by narrowing your search. Many times, buyers become let down after touring properties based on what they thought they could get a loan for, only to be told they do not qualify for as much as they assumed. Basically, they spent time viewing properties they cannot afford and anything they look at now will disappointing in comparison.

Your buying power is most likely a decision you will make with your bank or lender, unless you are paying cash. Financing a condominium is not the same as lending on a house. If your lender has approved you for a loan it does not a mean the condo you want to purchase is approved. The lender underwriting policies for condos are different and more complicated than regular residential homes. Conventional, VA and FHA all have their own guidelines for approval. Unless you are going to pay cash, it is recommended you work with an experienced condo Realtor and lender who know the process. For experienced condo lenders, please go to www.CondoLivingDallas.com to find someone that matches your needs.

One difference with association living is that lending institutions take into consideration the financial stability of the developer and/or the association, depending on the stage of the project. This and details on loan fees, closing costs, and escrow will be covered in Chapter 6.

Once a bank or lender qualifies you for a certain amount, you can use this information to determine your monthly payments. When calculating this payment, you will consider taxes and insurance to determine how the total fits into your budget. For taxes and insurance information go to www.CondoLivingDallas.com for links to county assessor websites and mortgage and insurance calculators and referrals. This will help you estimate taxes and insurance based on your loan amount.

Be sure to add in the association fee you will be charged monthly, quarterly, or yearly. Association fees can differ dramatically from one development to another, depending on the number of units, amenities, size of the unit, and whether utilities are included. The association fee is an important factor to consider when calculating your projected monthly mortgage payment.

Choosing A Style

The next question to answer is what style of association living you prefer — high rise condominium, townhome, condominium, or zero lot line? After reading in Chapter 2 about the differences among the three, you have probably already decided. High rise condominiums are more suited to downtown due to the space limitations, but you can usually find a townhome or condominium close to all downtown action, if that's your preference. Zero lot lines, townhomes and condominiums are often found in the surrounding DFW areas. If you decided on a high-rise condominium, you still have more decisions to make. High-rise condominiums really come in three different types — new construction, conversion of apartment buildings, and conversion of old warehouse-type buildings.

A conversion is when a developer buys an old apartment building or warehouse and converts it into condominium units. Some developers will completely gut the building leaving only a structural shell and modernize the entire facility, including electricity and plumbing infrastructure. Others will only repaint the walls and install some new appliances.

When buying a unit in a converted apartment or old warehouse, determine to what extent the building has been modernized. A list of questions in Chapter 5 will guide you through this process.

In a new building, you will usually get a one-year builder's warranty on everything in your unit, such as appliances, flooring, HVAC, etc. If you buy into the property early at a reduced price, you may benefit from some quick appreciation along with low tax assessments due to the absence of a history upon which to base its value.

A new building does not, however, guarantee the absence of problems. A poorly planned development may end up in bankruptcy due to slow sales, creating unhappy clients and a bad reputation. Also, units that are built today may not have the same quality of construction as some of the older, proven buildings. It may take years for problems to surface due to poor building practices.

HINT: *I always recommend that you get a resume from the developer of successful past projects. Good developers want to meet potential buyers. Your Realtor can make these arrangements.*

While it's nice to buy in a new building where everything is new and shiny, and old building already has history and has proved its worth. Some people prefer a new building, others will only settle for the exposed brick and high ceilings found only in older converted buildings. Whatever your preference, you still need to ask the questions in Chapter 5. The answers will help you protect your investment.

Use Value vs. Cash Value

Getting the most for your money is usually the driving motivation when looking for the right real estate investment. This is called cash value. You are placing a value on the amount of return you expect to get on your purchase. Buy low now so you can sell at a higher price later, hope for a climbing economy that will support an aggressive appreciation style, and then you can start planning what to do with all the money you are going to make when you eventually sell, right?

Let's face it, the market is not set up that way and will never support this perfect ideal. If that scenario worked, all home owners you know would eventually be rich. Sure, everyone knows someone who bought in a buyer's market and later sold in a seller's market, making a substantial gain. Many people in the DFW market who bought 2008-2012 and are selling now are making those appreciation gains. But consider this: if they sold in a seller's market, they usually have to buy again right away in a seller's market — which offsets any gain. On the other hand, purchasing a home in a buyer's market is great for investors who are looking for rental property as they will have someone else paying the bills, so they can later capitalize on the appreciation.

HINT: *Historically in the condominium business, the best time to get a better deal is early in the construction process. That's when the developer is anxious to sell a few units to create the perception that his condominium units are in demand.*

Unless you find a really desperate seller who needs to sell fast, for whatever reason, you will probably end up paying market value like the rest of us. Ninety-eight percent of residential purchases are at market value — that puts you on the same playing field as everyone else.

It's a common and accepted practice in residential real estate to make an offer lower than the asking price. If the seller doesn't like the offer, he can always counter with terms more to his liking. Negotiations go back and forth between the buyer and seller until the price and terms are acceptable to both parties. This is how market value is determined. Sellers have a general idea of what their property is worth and, unless they are under some undue pressure, they are going to stick to that price.

> "Wealth is the ability to fully experience life."
> - *Henry David Thoreau*

Now let's look at the difference between cash value and use value. The home of my dreams will have a large kitchen with lots of counter space because I like to cook with fresh produce and need a large prep area. The sink will be close to the stove, so I don't have to carry hot and dirty cookware across the kitchen floor. I'll want a large pantry and a high ceiling for hanging my pots and pans. I don't want a dishwasher as I like to do my dishes right after a meal, plus it takes up valuable cabinet space.

This and a few other minor items, and I will have the kitchen of my dreams. I think you get my point, which is that the use value of a house that fits my lifestyle is worth at least market value to me. I wouldn't break the deal over a few thousand dollars because I want to win over on the seller and get the buy of the century. Sometimes quality of life is worth paying for. This functionality or use value would make living in this house not only fun but efficient for me. I could be happy in this house for a long time and if minor things about the house need changing, I can do that over time.

Finding a condominium that fits your needs and improves your quality of life offers tremendous use value to you for years to come. I've had several potential buyers look at more than 20-30 homes over a period of time to find the perfect fit, only to get their hearts broken because they made a low-ball offer and got beat out by a buyer with a more reasonable offer. Imagine losing your dream condo over a few thousand dollars. I have had buyers who, after losing the deal, wanted to come back with a higher offer for the condominium they loved, but it was too late.

Think about use value and what it means to you. A maintenance free lifestyle has a major impact on quality of life and is a major attraction of condominium living. But take it a step further to see how functional a unit is to you personally. Imagine yourself working in the kitchen, taking out the trash, doing laundry. Are the master bedroom, closet and bathroom functional for you and your family? Determining use value in your price range will help you live happily every day you own that condo.

Appreciation

Most buyers ask me, "How much will this property appreciate in the next few years?" My answer is always, "I don't know." Condominiums appreciate or depreciate for various reasons.

Is the condominium well-kept with freshly painted and clean entryways and a well-kept exterior? Are lawns mowed, landscape well groomed, and parking areas in good repair? Is the location experiencing consistent neighborhood improvements? How are the schools in the area? Are there more private schools than public schools? Is the association maintaining adequate financial reserve for potential emergencies, plus setting money aside for normal wear and tear? Then, barring any 9/11 type disaster or The Great Recession experienced a few years ago this condominium should experience 3-6% appreciation per year on average.

Appreciation may edge upwards if the condominium is located in an area that is seeing tremendous improvements. Improvements that lend themselves to economic growth include job growth, new corporate relocations, public railways, cultural attractions, new grocery stores, retail stores, theatres, and hotels, plus updating of older buildings and parking lots. With these improvements and assuming everything else is in check, then you can expect higher than normal appreciation. All of these economic indicators are currently happening in DFW.

HINT: *Do not rely on rumors or even the newspaper or news stations for adequate information on neighborhood developments. Instead talk to the city planners or area associations. They can tell you what projects investors are planning. For contact information, go to www.CondoLivingDallas.com.*

The bottom line in any buying decision is your comfort level. Chapter 5 details questions you should ask before making a buying decision.

Chapter 5 — Get Informed

Questions to Ask Before Signing on the Dotted Line

Below is a list of questions that will help you become a highly informed buyer. As you will discover, no two condominium associations operate the same way (even with the same association managing two different properties), and not all will have what you want. Asking these questions helps you avoid buying what you don't want. A good Realtor will help you get the answers you need to guide you toward making the right purchase.

Amenities

- Is there a business center, club house, and or community room? If so, who is allowed to use these rooms and will the association be responsible for upkeep?
- Is there a deposit required?
- Is there a movie theatre? If so, who is allowed to use it and how is it scheduled?
- Are there separate laundry facilities?
- Is there a separate wine cellar space and is it for sale or lease?
- Is there a roof top deck? If so, is it residents only?
- Does the association provide for plants and deck furniture?
- Will the association provide a gas grill, or are grills prohibited?
- Is there a concierge service? What are the hours? What services will they provide?
- Is there a valet service? What are there hours? What services do they provide?
- Is there a full-time maintenance person? Does the maintenance person live on site? Will he or she be

available for unit owner repairs or does he maintain the building and space only? Is he available for emergencies 24/7?

Security

- Is there going to be a full or part-time security person on site?
- How do I get in touch with security?
- Does the main entrance have security?
- Do the parking areas and exterior of the building have security cameras?
- Are there security cameras on the individual floors?
- Does the lobby have security cameras?
- Does the elevator have a security system that restricts entrance to different locations?
- Can owners have security systems installed in their individual units?

New Construction

- Has the developer built condominiums before? If so, where and when?
- Does the developer provide a one-year home builders warranty? What does it cover? What does it not cover? (ceiling fans, HVAC, doors, etc.)
- What are the standards for finishes?
- What are the upgrades? (floors, countertops, paint colors, etc.)
- Is a washer and dryer included?
- Is the refrigerator included?
- How long does it take to finish out a unit?
- Does the purchase provide for a free consultation with an interior designer?

Association Fees

- What do the fees cover?
- What utilities do they cover? (gas, electric, sewer, water, cable, trash, internet)
- What is the monthly fee?
- What is the monthly fee per square foot?
- Are the fees expected to go up in the next year?
- Are there currently any special assessments?
- Is there any pending litigation?
- What is the grace period for a late payment or no payment?
- When was the last time the fees were raised?

Parking

- Is there a garage, covered, surface, or street parking?
- Is the garage parking heated or air conditioned?
- Have any repairs been made to the parking structure?
- How many parking units come with the units?
- Is there associated storage with any of the parking spaces?
- Does the association own the parking structure?
- Is there a separate fee for parking and its maintenance?
- Can I sell my parking spot?
- Are parking spots purchased or leased?
- Is there any extra parking available for sale or lease?
- If spots are not purchased or leased, are they assigned?
- Is there a maximum number of vehicles allowed per residence?

- Are residents allowed to do any maintenance on their own vehicles on site?
- Are campers, RVs, boats, or trailers allowed?
- What is not permitted?
- Are garage or yard sales permitted?

Trash

- Is there recycling?
- Is there a trash chute on each floor?
- On what day is trash picked up?
- Is there a trash porter?

Unit

- Can I operate a business out of my unit?
- Is there a limit on how many people may occupy a residence?
- May I rent my unit out?
- Is there any limitation on length of the rental (six month or a year)?
- Do renters need to be approved by the board?
- Are there any rules associated with renting?
- Can you do short term rentals?
- Is signage allowed? (rental or for sale signs)
- Are there laundry facilities in each unit?
- Are there limitations on holiday decorations?
- How is the square footage measured?
- Are balconies included in the sellable square footage?

Storage

- How much storage is available per unit?
- Is more storage available for sale or rent?
- Can I rent out my storage?
- Is the storage climate controlled?

- Is there bicycle storage?

Landscape

- Is there room for a vegetable or flower garden that I maintain?
- Are flowers and plants allowed outside of the unit?
- Can I put up holiday decorations?

Architectural

- What items may be attached to the building's exterior?
- What are the rules for patios, decks, window treatments, satellite dishes, skylights, fences, doors, outside living areas, pool area, exterior lighting and decorations?
- Is there an architectural committee or board that must approve alterations?
- Is there an engineer to approve maintenance of HVAC, water heater, etc.
- What is the procedure?

Pets

- What are the limitations on pets?
- Is there a weight or number restriction?
- What kinds of pets are prohibited?
- Is there a walking area?
- What is the leash requirement?
- Who handles pet complaints?
- Does an architectural committee need to be informed of a doggy door installation?

Quiet Enjoyment

- What is the procedure for noise complaints?
- What is the penalty for excessive noise?

- Do the party walls separating each unit meet the current code?
- Have there been complaints regarding noise between units?
- Is there extra sound proofing under the flooring or in the walls or ceilings?
- Are there requirements for the type of flooring that can be used for a second, third, fourth, etc. floor unit for sound?

Balcony

- Does the unit come with a balcony?
- Is there a weight restriction for the balcony?
- Are gas grills allowed?
- Are decorations allowed?
- Who is responsible for repairs of the balcony?
- How will bird infestations and droppings be dealt with?
- Is the balcony owned by the resident or the HOA?
- Is the balcony square footage included as saleable square feet?
- Is the balcony included as taxable square feet?

Building Information

- Does the association own the entire building and the land?
- If the land is leased, when is the lease up?
- Is parking owned by the association?
- When was the building built?
- How many floors are there?
- How many units are there in the building?
- How many units are rentals?
- What is the name of the developer?

- If it is a conversion, when was it converted?
- How extensive was the conversion?
- Were the utilities replaced from the street and throughout the building?
- Was the building gutted before being converted?
- Was the insulation replaced throughout the building?
- Were the sewer and water lines replaced throughout the building?
- Was all the electrical replaced?
- Were new energy-efficient soundproof windows installed?
- Were party walls between units rebuilt with extra sound proofing?
- Is there a recent building inspection report available for review?

Guests

- Is there special parking for guests?
- Is there a guest suite available to rent?
- Is there a limit to how long guests may stay?

Rentals

- See Chapter 7 on Rentals

Budget

- How often is the budget reviewed?
- When is it prepared?
- How has the budget compared to actual expenses for the last 3 years?
- What is done with any excess money at the end of the year?
- What happens if there is a shortage at the end of the year?

- How much money is put into the contingency fund each year?
- How much money is in the contingency fund now?
- Have there been any special assessments in the last 3 years?
- Are there any special assessments due at this time?

Financial Documents

- Is the following information available to you before you buy?
    - A statement of budget amounts versus actual expenses?
    - A copy of current month's balance sheet?
    - A copy of the current month's profit and loss statement?
    - A copy of the independent CPA audit for the last fiscal year?
    - Percentage of the owner's assessments that are put into a reserve fund?
    - Current balance in the reserve fund?
    - Copy of the last reserve study
- Are funds being replaced as per the reserve study?
- Name of the institution that holds the association funds?
- What is the investment strategy?

Recreational Amenities

- Is there a swimming pool?
    - Is it owned and managed by the association?
    - Are there any extra fees for using the swimming pool?
    - Any limitations to number of guests?
- Is there a fitness center?

- o Is it owned and managed by the association?
- o Are there any extra fees for using the fitness center?
- o Any limitations to number of the guests?
- Is there a tennis court?
  - o Is it owned and managed by the association?
  - o Are there extra fees for using the tennis court?
- Is there a clubhouse?
  - o Is it owned and managed by the association?
  - o Are there any extra fees for the clubhouse?

Management Company

- How long has the company managed the association?
- What services does the company perform for the association?
- Does the company attend all association and board meetings?
- Does the company have extra fees for other services provided by the residents?
- Is there an emergency contact?
- Is there a specific manager associated with the property?

Chapter 6 — The Purchase Process

A Realtor's Guidance

Go into the selection and purchase of your unit with expertise on your side by working with a Realtor who is a condominium specialist. The best way to explain what a REALTOR who specializes in condominiums provides is to describe how I operate. As a real estate agent, I assist clients with finding a condominium that fits their lifestyle and needs.

We start by sitting down and talking about what is important to them. I ask a lot of questions about location, finishes, parking, amenities, price range, square footage, number of bedrooms, etc. By getting to know my clients' needs and lifestyles, I can save them a tremendous amount of time by matching them with a particular community and the amenities they want.

As a buyer's representative, I can also provide information that a salesperson or developer might avoid. For example, I can tell you if noise form street traffic at a particular time of day is an issue, or if the sound proofing is not sufficient. I can also clue you in if the project is saturated with rentals, a new building is scheduled to be built that will block the unit's view, or the area around the condominium complex has experienced excessive crime.

One of the most important lessons I have learned is to make sure my clients have seen everything available in their price range. Buying a home is process of elimination, not a selection process. Once this is done and they have narrowed the search, then I provide more detail regarding the condominium and financial documents. Many times, buyers are so focused on the location and unit itself that they overlook the details of the condominium as well as financial documents and issues such as condominium insurance and whether a condominium can be financed.

Those details are important, so I make sure buyers are fully informed. Because my role as a Realtor is to protect the buyer's investment, I also do a market analysis to make sure the buyer does not purchase an overpriced property.

> "Real estate cannot be lost or stolen, nor can it be carried away. Purchased with common sense, paid for in full, and managed with reasonable care, it is about the safest investment in the world."
> *-Franklin D Roosevelt, 32nd U.S. President*

Buyer's agents are legally obligated to:

- Not disclose confidential information
- Act fairly and honestly
- Seek a price and terms which are acceptable
- Promote the interest of the buyer with the utmost faith, loyalty and fidelity
- Account for all monies
- Disclose, in writing, all adverse material facts
- Advise to obtain expert advice on matters beyond a REALTOR's expertise
- Comply with all applicable federal, state, and local statutes, rules and ordinances

In addition, I guide buyers through the purchase agreement, negotiate a price and terms for the buyer's benefit, and help with pre-approval for a mortgage. I also coordinate the appraisal, title work, moving plans, home warranty, home owner's insurance, home inspections, escrow closing, and taking possession. I ensure the paperwork is completed properly and efficiently. It is a before, during and after process for each purchase agreement for the buyers when working together with me.

The most important part of what a REALTOR does is help buyers understand what is happening and protect them throughout the process. Buying a condominium is not only a big investment, it's also a lifestyle offered by condominium/community association living. The best way to do that is to make sure buyers are informed and prepared.

The Purchase Agreement

Are you ready to sign a purchase agreement? Do you have answers to all your questions? Do you have a good understanding of the condominium's documents and financials? Have you visited the property numerous times to get a feel for the neighborhood? Have you dealt with the developer or sales staff without feeling pressured? Have you interviewed owners in the building? Have you reviewed the market analysis? If so, you're ready to sign a contract to purchase the property you've selected.

> "People are usually the happiest at home."
> -*William Shakespeare, British Playwright*

Purchase agreement contracts vary from place to place, but all are basically built on a foundation of standard and required legal verbiage. Newly constructed condominiums or newly converted condominiums may be a little more involved so as to protect the developer's interests. Keep in mind the developers have invested a tremendous amount of time and money and will want the purchase to go as smoothly as possible, while protecting themselves from any unreasonable circumstances.

All purchase contracts have many necessary and basic elements. These include:

- How the title will be conveyed
- The amount of the purchase
- Proration of any assessments
- Proration of taxes
- Choice of title company
- Survey requirements
- Seller's disclosure statement
- Estimate of costs
- Home warranty
- Home inspection days and money
- Earnest Money amount
- Lead based paint addendum if necessary
- Earnest and option money receipts
- Executed date
- Third Party Financing addendum if needed

These are standard, and your REALTOR can explain in detail how each of these pertains to you.

Conditions and Contingencies

Contingencies and conditions are contractual elements that affect you more than any of the standard legalese above. This is where the contracts get creative and give buyers the option to back out if conditions are not fulfilled to the buyer's satisfaction. Some basic contingencies are as follows:

- This contract is contingent on my attorney reviewing all condominium documents and financials

- This contract is contingent on the buyer getting final approval for FHA financing

- This contract is contingent on the results of a property inspection

- This contract is contingent on buyer making final selections for final finishes (for new construction)

- This contract is contingent on buyer selling their current home

- This contract is contingent on buyer accepting a new job

- This contract is contingent on buyer getting relocated by employer

- This contract is contingent on probate releasing funds to the buyer

- This contract is contingent on finalization of buyer's divorce

As you can see, contingencies can be written for just about anything. Remember if contingencies are met, you are legally obligated to buy. Sellers do not have to agree to any contingency. If they suspect you are not serious, sellers can counter with a modification to your contingency or reject the contract all together.

Once an offer is accepted, then the condominium is taken off the market for sale. If the contingency is such that it will take the condominium off the market for a longer than normal period of time, such as waiting for your house to sell, then the seller may accept the offer with the option to keep the condominium on the market and give you a 48 hour right of first refusal if another offer comes in. This is often called an Active Kick Out contract.

Keep in mind price is not the only way to negotiate a contract. You can ask for the seller to cover some, if not all, of your closing costs. Often times closing costs are a result of inspections and to cover the cost of needed repairs. You can also ask the sellers to pay for one year of association dues.

Most likely, the seller will counter your offer with some adjustments to your conditions. That's why we call it negotiations. Developers of new projects, however, leave very little leeway in their pricing for negotiation.

Estimated Buyer Sheet

In addition to preparing a purchase agreement, your REALTOR will also prepare an estimated buyer sheet. This gives you an idea estimate of what all your closing costs will be, along with an estimate of your monthly payment including taxes, insurance, and monthly association fee. This information is important because it determines approximately how much it will cost you to close on your purchase. Below is a sample of an estimated buyer sheet for a $300,000 purchase:

ESTIMATED CLOSING COST

LENDER FEES

Down Payment (5%)	$15,000
Loan processing fee*	$495
Underwriting fee	$595

THIRD PARTY FEES

Loan Appraisal	$465-500
Home Warranty	$550

TITLE FEES

Document Preparation	$415
Closing/Escrow Fee	$400

Owners Title Insurance	$1900
Title Courier Fee	$60
Title Endorsements	$175
Title Guaranty Assessments	$4.50
Title Survey**	$400-500
Mortgage Recording Charge	$160
Sub Total	**$20,619.50**

CLOSING COSTS AND PREPAIDS	
Earnest Money Deposit	$3,000
First Year's Homeowners Insurance	$2,100
Home Inspection	$450
Termite Inspection	$75
Total Prior to Closing	**$5,625**

ESTIMATED MONTHLY PAYMENT	
Principal and interest (5%, 30 year fixed)	$1,530
Association fee*** (.20 per sq. ft. on 1,500 sq. ft. total)	$300
Monthly Tax	$587
Monthly Insurance	$175
Total Monthly Payment	**$2,592**

*Varies by bank and type of loan, remember to add to total

**Only condominiums that need a survey are Townhomes, Zero Lot Lines and Single Family Attached.

***Fees can vary anywhere from .20 to .40 cents per square foot depending on what's included in the association fees. Also, most associations cover a blanket insurance.

These figures are only estimates and will change from bank to bank, type of inspection, home warranty, insurance company, and accuracy of the tax assessment.

Contract Negotiations

The negotiation process starts with the buyer making an offer that's lower than the asking price, expecting either an acceptance or counteroffer. This back and forth game goes on until the terms and conditions are acceptable to both parties.

Sellers typically have a no-lower-than figure in mind when selling their condominiums, but of course would like to get as close as possible to the asking price. Negotiating for better than the asking price is part of the game and the seller will expect it.

The part of negotiating that is totally unacceptable is when a buyer tries to bully or beat down the seller by playing the I won/you lost game. This approach is based on greed and by no means makes the world a better place.

A buyer's market, when the supply of condominiums is greater than the demand, is generally considered a good time to buy. An excess of condominiums on the market creates more competition, forcing sellers to lower their prices. However, this does not automatically mean the seller is desperate and is able or willing to take a lower-than-market value offer.

For example, the seller may be upside down (owe more than the property is worth) due to refinancing when home values were at a peak and/or have maxed out a home equity line. In this case, the seller's bottom line may be more than you are willing to pay because the seller's price is driven by his current loan amount and not fair market value.

Negotiating with a seller in this situation can be frustrating, especially if you really love the condominium. At this point you have to compare use value with cash value, as discussed in Chapter 4, to determine if the property is worth the extra money the seller is asking.

Sometimes a seller will be forced to sell due to some unforeseen circumstances and will have to take a loss and write a check at closing to cover the difference between sales price and loan amount. This does happen and is made worse if the seller has a prepayment penalty clause on his current loan.

Sellers are motivated to sell for various reasons — job change, getting away from the heat, retirement, upgrading to a larger home, change of neighborhoods, loss of a loved one, change of school for kids, etc. Add these motivations to the seller's financial circumstances, and you can see what you are up against.

The best scenario is when the seller has very little debt or the condominium is paid for. In this case, the seller has more room to negotiate and is in a better position to pay for some of the closing costs.

In any case, the seller's goal is to get you pay as close to the asking price as possible. The buyer wants to pay as close as possible to the seller's bottom figure. Once you have reached an agreeable number, you're ready for the next step.

In a seller's market, which means inventory is less than 6 months, buyers often face multiple offer situations. In this case the buyer is forced to submit their highest and best offer or move on. However, when an area is in a seller's market a buyer often "kicks the can down the road" and will face the same multiple offer situation on the next condominium. This is often the case when competing against at least one other buyer and there can be as many as 5, 10, or 15 plus buyers to compete against.

Hint: Every complex is different and price, location, and desire to purchase from a buyer are major contributors in multiple offer situations. Ask your Realtor what the complex inventory is for your unit. If the Realtor responds with seller's market it is below a 6-month inventory while if it is above 6 months it is a buyer's market.

The Inspection

Even though you have made several visits to your new condominium it is now time to have a professional give it a far more in-depth look. This is one of the conditions of the purchase agreement. You have a set number of days (usually 5-10 days) after the acceptance of the contract to have a professional licensed inspector look at the property or inspect yourself. Your goal is to determine whether this property's condition is as good as you initially believed.

Hiring a licensed inspector is not an everyday event, so most buyers rely on a recommendation. Your Realtor works with licensed inspectors almost daily and can guide you to someone who is experienced with condominiums.

An inspector's job is to ensure the building is structurally sound and all major systems are in good working order. I have worked with some really great inspectors. I've also worked with some who seem intent on causing unnecessary concern — enough to unfortunately break the deal. These inspectors are determined to justify their existence by pole vaulting over ant hills and eventually find themselves unemployed. A professional inspector looks for potential problems that could cost you a lot of money later on. To find a reliable inspector, go to www.CondoLivingDallas.com. The following is a standard checklist for inspectors:

- Chimneys
- Skylights
- Gutters
- Flashings
- Roof
- Doors and windows
- Wood Decks
- Porches and Patios
- Foundations
- Driveway's
- Retaining Walls
- Sprinkler Systems
- Attics
- Garage
- Insulation
- Ventilation
- Walls and Ceilings and Floors
- Stairs and railings
- Kitchen Appliances
- Water Seepage
- Heating and Air Conditioning
- Plumbing
- Water Heaters
- Electrical

Some of these will apply more to a townhome condominium than a high-rise condominium. The point is to have your inspector give you his professional opinion in terms of overall structure of the building and common areas.

HINT: Some condominiums have old boiler-system heaters. A failed heater can be a tremendous burden on an association's financial reserves. If your inspector's report mentions an outdated boiler or related problems, review the associa-

tion's budget to see if money is set aside for such an expense. If not, you can expect to pay a special assessment when major repairs are needed. If the budget has been properly managed, there will be ongoing contributions to an emergency and contingency fund for such expenses. Also make sure to ask the board for any recent building inspection reports.

A newly constructed condominium has to pass city inspections, so it would seem that an inspector is not needed. But not all developers are alike and unfortunately some are questionable, even if an inspection was performed during construction to ensure the building met standards. No matter what you're buying, an inspector will provide reliable information, so you can purchase a condominium with confidence.

After the inspection is complete, you will receive a detailed report of findings. These are ranked from serious to minor. One of 4 things will happen at this point:

1. You are not concerned with the findings on the report and would like to purchase the property.

2. The report reveals some major defects and you would like the seller to repair them at his own cost before you purchase the property.

3. Buyer can request either closing costs or price reduction in lieu of repairs from seller.

4. The report revealed major defects and you would like to terminate the contract.

If option 2 or 3 is selected, then the seller normally has 24 hours to respond in writing to notify buyer what steps, if any, the seller will take to correct major defects before closing. Sellers are usually very willing to work with the buyer in repairing major defects or with closing costs or price reduction in lieu of repairs.

HINT: *Get proof and receipt of repairs prior to closing.*

The Home Warranty

More than half of all home buyers have had two major items fail in the first year of ownership. The home warranty provides peace of mind by eliminating the uncertainty of unexpected home repair bills.

Warranties are usually good for one year after the closing date and cover air conditioning, heating systems, electrical, plumbing, refrigerator, oven, range, dishwasher, microwave, water heater, garage door openers, locks, washer and dryer, disposal, etc.

Home Warranties normally cost around $500 and require you to pay a deductible for any service call. So, if your furnace needs to be replaced, all you pay is the deductible — usually around $75.

If you are buying new construction, a home warranty is not needed as a one-year builders' warranty is usually provided by the developer. New construction warranties are generally longer than one year on many of the items such as foundation, HVAC, plumbing, electrical, and roof. This should be stated in the purchase agreement. To find a reputable home warranty company, please go to www.CondoLivingDallas.com.

Insurance

In community style living, the association's insurance coverage should cover the following:

- *Property* — Protects the property against loss from theft, fire, or other perils.

- *Liability* — Covers accidental or unintentional injuries on your premises and unintentional damage to other people's property.

- *Umbrella (Blanket Insurance)* — Gives an added layer of insurance above and beyond your association's coverage.

  HINT: *Umbrella insurance is often covered within your HOA coverage.*

- *Crime* — Provides for the perils of burglary, theft, and robbery.

- *Director and Officer* — This errors and omissions insurance protects the association from legal consequences of decisions and actions made by the board.

The extent of coverage each association's policy provides depends on the size and scope of the development. If it includes a lot of common areas and amenities — especially pools, tennis courts, spas, work out facilities, community rooms, etc. — then the amount will go up very quickly.

Despite all this coverage, you are still responsible for insuring your own personal property, personal liability, and guests' medical coverage. No one insurance program fits every condominium owner's needs, and every condominium development will have variations to the above insurance coverage. The trick is to find an insurance policy that matches up to the association's policy and still gives you plenty of coverage. Finding a component insurance agent who specializes in condominiums is imperative. For agents I endorse, go to www.CondoLivingDallas.com.

The Walk Through

No more than 48 hours before closing on the purchase of your condominium, you will do a walkthrough of your unit. This is for several reasons: first to see if everything is repaired as agreed upon in the inspection report; second to check for any damage to the property since the last visit; third, if you're buying new construction, this is the time to create a punch list of items that need to be finished.

A new construction punch list checks for the following:

- Flooring is without nicks or scratches and wood has no bubbled areas.

- Base boards and trim boards fit properly, and nail holes are covered.

- Walls are smooth and without scratches or dents.

- Every cabinet door has a proper seal.

- Sinks and faucets are not scratched, and handles are aligned.

- Ceramic tiles on the floors or walls match up evenly and are fully grouted.

- Doors open and close smoothly and seal properly.

- Windows open and close.

- Ceilings fans are balanced.

- Kitchen counter tops have finished edges and no excessive gaps.

Punch list has historically been the biggest complaint when buying new construction. I have known some buyers who have waited up to a year to get all the items on the list repaired. Because contractors do make errors, especially when they are rushed, there will always be items that need to be repaired. Something as simple as bringing a dishwasher into the unit for installation can end with the floor being scratched.

HINT: If you are one of the last buyers in a complex and the developer has moved onto the next project, it is imperative to get the punch list items completed immediately and get the developer to agree to the repairs in writing and that they will be completed by a certain date.

The Closing

Closing is done with a Title Company in the state of Texas. That's where you will sign all the necessary documents. Before closing you will be given a document with final figures for closing costs. If something has changed in the loan or the down payments, for example, then the numbers will reflect that. These totals on the closing disclosure form determine how much money you need to bring in order to close and legally take possession of your new condominium. This payment must be in the form of a cashier's check or bank wire, which is the most preferred form.

Once documents are signed and the money exchanges hands and the you hear the word funding, you can finally take possession of the property you have worked so hard to buy. You can start enjoying your new lifestyle with the confidence that you've made the right decision.

As you can see, a REALTOR who specializes in condominiums knows what details to consider between first look and funding. The best news is it costs you nothing to have someone with experience looking out for your interests. This is what I do and the reason for this book. If you would like my help, feel free to visit www.CondoLivingDallas.com or call me at 214-552-9304.

Chapter 7 — Condominiums as Rental Properties

Condominiums Are Smart Rentals

Becoming a landlord by purchasing single-family homes is an incredible amount of work and risk. There are countless stories of tenants destroying properties, then skipping out on rent —leaving the landlord high and dry. In addition to not paying rent these tenants sometimes trash the place and the landlord is left facing thousands of dollars in repairs before the house can be rented again. Add this to the normal expense of maintaining the exterior of the building, landscape maintenance, and garage upkeep, and you can see why most investors stay away from this type of real estate as a source of income.

What if you could invest in an income-producing property with minimum hassle? That's right better tenants, no building maintenance, no landscaping to take care of, and someone else to enforce reasonable rules and regulations.

By buying a condominium unit as a rental, you are taking on another party who will do all this for you because the condominium's association, its board of directors, and your tenant's neighbors will monitor your tenant's behavior. If behavior is out of line, the board will address it. Now add the fact that all the exterior maintenance is covered by the association — and possibly some of the utilities — and you have a landlord's dream come true.

Here is another perk: Condominiums attract better tenants. Think about it. If you were a person who wanted to throw a wild party and live a lifestyle that is not conducive to community living, you would most likely choose a single-family home where you could not only invite all your rowdy friends over but have them live with you as well.

> "It's tangible, it's solid, it's beautiful. It's artistic, from my standpoint, and I just love real estate."
> -*Donald Trump, president and real estate tycoon*

An organized association with rules and regulations will usually deter this group of renters. Condominiums just don't attract this type of tenant. Instead you will attract people who would prefer to live in a building that provides not only physical security but also the security that rules and regulations provide.

If you're interested in this type of investment, remember that not all condominiums are run the same. This is a very important part of the selection process. Make sure the association is strong and the board is effective in managing its affairs. Most condominium associations are well run because board members are usually residents who want to protect their investment.

Return on Your Investment

For years, a rule of thumb for setting rental price was 1 percent of property value — one month's rent should 1 percent of the purchase price. A $200,000 condominium for example would then rent for $2000. This rule considered some very nice cash flow as a return on your investment. Unfortunately, the property values in most areas have exceeded rents significantly. A $200,000 condominium will most likely bring anywhere from $1500- $2200 in monthly rent, depending on location and amenities. With the addition of the association fees you could easily be into a negative cash flow situation.

This does not necessarily mean that it's a bad investment. If you look at the whole picture, you will see that cash flows adjust as years go by, along with beneficial factors such as appreciation, depreciation, and the accumulation of tax-free equity. Here's an example of how the numbers break down:

$200,000 purchase price
-$40,000 down payment
$160,000 loan amount

$1200 Monthly principal and interest payment
$388 Monthly property tax
$50 Monthly insurance
$300 Monthly condominium assessment fee
$1938 Total monthly expenses

Let's say, for example, that this investment brings in a negative cash flow of $38 per month from a $1900 rent. At first glance, it would appear to be a foolish thing to do. But, lets calculate it all the way through. Rental properties provide four opportunities for a gain:

- Appreciation
- Depreciation
- Building of Equity
- Cash Flow

Appreciation

Because of the popularity of condominiums as a lifestyle, the trend is that appreciation rates are exceeding single family houses. Downtown areas generally will have the best appreciation for condominiums compared to surrounding areas. But for arguments sake, let's assume a worst-case scenario of a low 3 percent appreciation on the example above.

$200,000 x 3% = $6000

If your down payment was $40,000 then on appreciation alone you've realized a 15% return on the cash you invested.

$6,000 / $40,000 = 15%

Depreciation

You can deduct depreciation on your condominium rental just like you would a single-family home. When calculating depreciation for a condominium, you will need to separate your share of all the common areas. For example, of the $200,000 purchase price, roughly $40,000 is for your undivided ownership in the building and all the common areas. These common areas will most likely include covered parking areas, pool, clubhouse, tennis courts, etc. The $160,000 is yours to depreciate. It is assumed that your condominium will wear out completely in 27.5 years.

> $160,000/27.5=$5819
> $5,819 annual depreciation
> 35% tax bracket (total federal and state)
> $5,819*.35=$2,037 total tax savings
> $2,037/$40,000=5%

If your down payment was $40,000 then you realized a gain of an additional 5% from depreciation

Building of Equity

Each payment that is made will add tax free equity to your property, giving you more return on investment. Using the above $200,000 condominium and a $40,000 down payment, we have figured the payment to be $752 per month ($9024 a year). Part of this payment goes to pay interest and part of it is used to pay off the loan. The more you pay off the loan, the more of the condominium you own. This is called building equity. This equity is building your net worth, which until sold is a tax-free gain.

YEAR	TOTAL PAYMENTS	PRINCIPAL	INTEREST
1	$9,024	$1,947	$7,303

Your equity has grown by $1,947 the first year. With the $40,000 down payment, your gain would be almost a 4.8% return on investment.

Each month, the amount paid toward interest decreases and the amount applied toward principal increases until eventually your last payment is all principal. Your return on investment for the fifth year will increase as follows:

YEAR	TOTAL PAYMENTS	PRINCIPAL	INTEREST
5	$9,024	$2,446	$6,831

With the $40,000 down payment, your return on investment for the fifth year has increased from 4.8% to 6.1%

Cash Flow

Cash flow is simple: the rental income minus the expenses.

RENTAL INCOME	
FIRST YEAR	$20,400
EXPENSES	
MORTGAGE PAYMENT	$9,024
INSURANCE	$1,000
TAXES	$4,656
ASSOCIATION DUES	$3,600
MAINTENANCE AND REPAIRS*	$300
MISCELLANEOUS**	$250
TOTAL EXPENSES	**$18,830**
NET INCOME	**$1,570**

*Remember, your association will cover most of your usual expenses.

**Some cities around the DFW metroplex require a leasing fee.

On a $40,000 down payment, this would be 10% return on investment.

Now let's pull it all together. Under the year columns are an accumulation of the years before it. For example, under five, the total of $31,854 is an accumulation of five years appreciation.

	1 YEAR	5 YEAR	10 YEAR	15 YEAR
APPRECIATION 3%	$6,000	$31,854	$68,782	$111,591
DEPRECIATION	$5,819	$29,095	$58,190	$87,285
CASH FLOW*	$1,570	$2.577	$4,113	$6,011
EQUITY	$1,947	$11,199	$25,272	$43,830
CUMULATIVE TOTALS	$15,336	$74,725	$156,357	$248,717

*Figured with a conservative annual 3% increase in rent and a 2% increase in expenses, giving a 1% increase in cash flow.

Numbers Tell the Story

These numbers are different for each project, although the principle will generally apply. As you can see appreciation has a huge impact on the return. The key is to find an area that will support some decent appreciation. An area of the city that has some long term projects, such as the Victory Park area with the American Airlines Center, Katy trail beginning, and connecting to the design district and Trinity River Project, colleges that are expanding their facilities like SMU and the area surrounding SMU (especially to the east in and around University and Lovers and in between Greenville and Skillman, which currently has some of the lowest values for condos inside the 635 loop), and the expansion of expressways are just a few. Get to know your city and look for these areas of positive growth.

The cash flow scenario above shows a running negative total and it is unlikely to continue to trend as rents do outgrow expenses at a faster rate than 1%. The numbers I used are quite conservative, so as not to inflate expectations.

To succeed in rentals, you have to take the time to plan for success. When negotiating, you have one shot to get it right. After the purchase, you are committed to work with what you bought. Make sure the numbers work in your favor before you buy. Base your purchase on the numbers and not on wishful thinking. Every year there is always a new crop of overanxious investors looking to make their million in real estate. Don't be afraid to walk away if the deal does not feel right.

If you have taken your time and done your homework, then you are on your way to being successful. Enjoy the ownership of maintenance free rental property.

If you would like to look at condominiums as investment properties, your first step is contacting an experienced Realtor who is plugged in to the local market. To connect with a condominium specialist, visit www.CondoLivingDallas.com or call 214-552-9304

Chapter 8 — Selling Your Condominium

How Condominium Sales Differ from Home Sales

One question potential condominium buyers ask is, "How easy will it be to sell my condominium if I get transferred or need to move?" The good news is that barring any unusual events, condominiums retain their value well.

However, selling your condominium is not the same as selling a house. A condominium is a unique item that that requires a different set of marketing skills.

A regular home is sold based on factors that apply to most houses. These are location, competition, timing, condition, and price. While these same factors apply to the sale of a condominium there are more factors to consider — especially the uniqueness of your particular unit and the amenities it offers.

Marketing Your Assets

The question to ask when marketing your unit is: why would someone want to buy my particular unit? The answers will help you create your marketing approach.

Consider this scenario: There is a development in Dallas that seems highly priced on initial investigation. In fact, it is priced higher than any other development in town. It is newly constructed and finished with quartz counter tops, maple wood cabinets, brand-name stainless steel appliances, beautifully finished maple wood flooring, and more.

Although these are nice finish outs, they're also simply becoming the standard for all the new condominium projects in town. What's even more curious is that the high-priced development has downsides, such as one parking spot per buyer compared to two with the competition. The competition also comes with a fireplace and a swimming pool while the high-priced condominium does not.

So how can this development justify the much higher per square foot price than all the other projects in town? How do they justify the price? Well, it's called creative marketing. The high-priced development's marketing goes something like this:

At our condominium you will experience the benefits of elegantly engineered living at its best. We don't provide a fireplace because we have discovered that space is too valuable, and a fireplace not only limits the way you arrange your furniture, it is also not compatible with large flat screen TVs and entertainment centers that have become so popular. But, if a fireplace is necessary to make your home more to your liking, we have configured each unit with gas lines for that purpose.

Our condominiums have the largest full-service fitness center attached to the building. This fitness center offers not only every piece of equipment available, it also has professional trainers, yoga, spin sessions and an executive club. We'll even do your laundry and have it ready for the next day's work out.

When you invite your friends to visit, you can have them park, in our spacious guest parking and take them up to the roof top community area for drinks and a view of the beautiful downtown Dallas skyline. Follow this up with a short walk to all of Dallas's finest restaurants, then stroll over to the movie theatre and enjoy a box office hit or take in one of the local gourmet coffee shops.

Need Groceries? We have 24-hour concierge service to order your groceries and have them in your suite ready to go at your convenience. If you have family visiting from out of town, reserve a room at the hotel next door and the Dart station is a short walk away. On the weekends you can take a walk on the Katy Trail or take in one of the weekend hockey, or basketball games at the American Airlines Center or catch any of the other number of other local entertainment activities.

All of this is within walking distance of some of the finest amenities that Dallas has to offer, and you didn't even have to start your car.

Did you notice the marketing pitch didn't even mention the unit's finishes or square footage? This condominium could be sold at a good price on just the amenities alone. So, the art of selling is to create value in everything you have to offer.

Internet Tools

The biggest marketing tool available today is the Internet. More than 90% of buyers today do their preliminary shopping online. Consider the historic percentages of people using the Internet for the home search process:

% OF PEOPLE USING THE INTERNET FOR THE HOME SEARCH PROCESS	
1995	2%
1999	37%
2000	50%
2002	60%
2005	78%
2007	90%

The few buyers who are still dedicated to shopping in the newspaper will eventually expand their searches to the Internet, so this is where you need maximum exposure.

In fact, just one website does not do the trick anymore because buyers come from many different angles when searching on the internet. I have more than 100 websites for posting the properties I list, including a personal website for each property.

When buyers find your property online, you have just a few seconds to WOW them with pictures and descriptions. Once you lure them in, they can read more detailed information and descriptions like the one above. Make it easy for buyers to find you by including a map plus written address. That's how you convince buyers to set up a showing appointment.

Signage

Most condominiums will not allow For Sale signs on the property for fear that signs will affect the aesthetic nature of the property. Sometimes the condominium's board of directors will work with you on this. Some even have certain size and color signs that can only be up for certain amount of time. If the board has a strict policy, you can at least put up a sign in the window. Keep it simple — For Sale and a phone number. Having a sign is helpful, but it's more important to have great Internet exposure.

Preparing Your Unit

Should you paint? My answer is YES! You will get one shot per potential buyer, so your unit better look like a Crate and Barrel advertisement. Old carpet should be replaced or at least cleaned and shampooed. If you have nice hardwood floors under the carpet, then trash the carpet and polish the floors. Chances are, buyers will like the hardwood floor better than your choice of carpet. And if they don't like hardwood floor, they have the option of installing new carpet themselves without having to tear out the old.

"Have nothing in your house that you don't know to be useful or believe to be beautiful."
-William Morris, British Artist

Easily fixable items should be repaired. Eliminate buyer objections by spending an afternoon making needed repairs on such items as door handles, loose hinges, dripping faucets, squeaky doors, etc.

I recommend removing about a third of your furniture, clearing off kitchen counters, and removing magnets from the refrigerator. A less cluttered look helps the buyer realize your unit's true potential because they can envision how their furniture will fit into the unit, instead of being overwhelmed with yours.

Before showing your unit, remember to look around and think Crate and Barrel — have freshly folded towels on the towel racks and fresh flowers on the kitchen table. Buyers get a feeling about a place the minute they walk in not only by what they see, but also by what they smell. Aromatherapy can have a huge impact on a buyer's impression. If you don't think smell has anything to do with a person's decision, just forget to clean out a cat box for a couple weeks and see how that makes you feel. You can turn the tide of someone's emotion by adding the scent of freshly baked cookies or by simmering a pot of apple cider and cinnamon.

Disclosure
Disclose, disclose, disclose. Fill out a property disclosure statement and be as honest as you can. This will pay off big time because buyers will see that you are up front and honest, and they will trust you. Buyers by nature are a little suspicious anyway, so any perceived deception will reduce your chances of a buyer taking a second look at your unit.

Besides the buyer will almost always hire an inspector on their behalf before they close on the property. You don't want to have to take your condominium off the market thinking you have it sold, only to have the deal fall apart because something you didn't disclose was found on the inspection. Not only are you disappointed, but you've also lost some valuable marketing time.

Setting Your Price

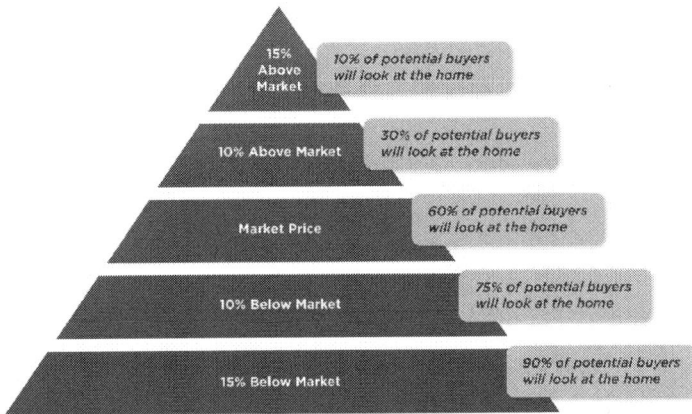

15% Above Market	10% of potential buyers will look at the home
10% Above Market	30% of potential buyers will look at the home
Market Price	60% of potential buyers will look at the home
10% Below Market	75% of potential buyers will look at the home
15% Below Market	90% of potential buyers will look at the home

If you want to sell your condominium, then price it to sell. Regardless of your circumstances, you will only get what a willing and able buyer can pay. If the property is too high in the beginning and sits for a period of time, then buyers will wonder what is wrong with it, delaying the sale of your unit.

If you decide to reduce the price after a lengthy period of time, it's usually too little, too late. The buyer's perception is their reality and your property has already been mentally marked as suspicious. On the other hand, you don't want to price your unit too low and lose out on income. However, in some markets it is advantageous to price at a lower price which can produce a multiple offers situation. This is when a property has more than one offer on the property. Generally, there are a couple of ways to handle this situation. One is to ask for highest and best offers by a certain date and time. The other is to work an individual offer. It is usually best to call for a highest and best offer as it generally leads to a price significantly higher than the asking price.

Pricing should be based on the market facts. This is one reason you should consider using a Realtor who specializes in condominiums — we have tools that provide updated sales information. In addition to historical data, a Realtor can compare your property against all the competing properties. Buyers interpret value based on recently sold and available properties in your neighborhood. Realtors who specialize in condominiums have that information at their fingertips.

You may have some great memories of special times with family and friends in your unit that are precious to you. Unfortunately, those memories mean nothing to potential buyers. A Realtor who is not emotionally involved can do a market analysis and determine the actual market value of your property.

Another benefit of hiring a professional is having marketing efforts match the property value. Your unit's market value may be $500,000, but if your marketing materials, flyers, Web sites, and the like are done cheaply then the price will seem too high.

For Sale by Owner

The for sale by owner generally has the mentality of saving money by not paying Realtor fees. With access to the internet, sellers can access websites that guide them in their for sale by owner process. That is fine, but the for sale by owner approach lacks the expertise of a real estate professional because we work with the market every day.

The advantage of using a Realtor who specializes in condominiums is the networking we do and of course our access to the Multiple Listing Service (MLS). There are close to 30,000 members in the Dallas and Ft. Worth area metroplex and surrounding areas that have access to the North Texas MLS, and there are over 6,000 brokerage offices that have access to the over 48,000 square miles the North Texas MLS covers. This is the best system for matching buyers with sellers. If a Realtor from Frisco has someone interested in a condominium in downtown Dallas, he or she will go to the MLS and search availability.

People who sell their condominiums without a Realtor often advertise in the newspaper, but this option is less popular because the response is not very good, and it is not cheap. Sellers can also pass out flyers to their friends or post a Facebook message but that is only helpful if your friends are interested in buying your unit.

The bottom line is this: Selling a condominium is time consuming. If you have the time and patience, it might be worth it. But if you don't have the time a Realtor has an array of marketing tools designed to help you be competitive and make your property available to everyone who is searching. Consider this: Realtors earn on average of up to 20% higher on sales price than a for sale by owner.

In fact, when selling a for sale by owner, six out of ten will eventually hire a Realtor after growing tired of the work involved or not getting any response. Two out of ten will actually sell their unit and the other two will completely give up and hire a Realtor at another time.

HINT: *It may be that you already have someone who is interested in buying your unit and you will not need a Realtor. In this case, I still recommend getting professional help with all the paperwork required to close the deal. A Realtor can guide you through this process at a reduced rate because money has not been tied up in marketing and showing your unit.*

Sellers often ask me about selling a home before it has gone on the market. My recommendation on this is usually no. Sometimes the seller thinks this will be a better deal. For a seller why not have thousands of people look at your home and have several people make offers rather than isolating it to one buyer. Why not have multiple buyers? This is almost always the best scenario and the best way to get the highest price possible for your unit.

Another question I get is this: Should I wait to sell my condominium until the market is favorable? Timing is really a personal decision and each person's circumstances are different. There is no one answer to this question as to when you should sell because, realistically, willing and able buyers are out there 12 months out of the year. Having said that, there are statistics showing that the spring and summer months are generally the best times for selling a property and the fall and winter months are the best time for buyers. So that covers the 12 months 😊

If you would like to have your property sold by an experienced Realtor, visit CondoLivingDallas.com or call 214-552-9304. We specialize in condominiums and provide one-stop shopping convenience for insurance, mortgage, title companies, relocation companies, moving professionals, and contractors.

Index

- Marketing Your Assets
- Internet Tools
- Signage
- Preparing Your Unit
- Disclosure
- Setting Your Price
- For Sale by Owner

Acknowledgements

If I were to acknowledge every soul that has blessed my life and helped to guide me to this endeavor, the book would be twice as long. I am overwhelmed with gratitude for so many kind helpful souls.

I would like to thank every family and individual who has trusted me to buy/sell/lease their home over the past 10 years. Serving allowed me the opportunity and experience to write this book.

I would like to thank Steve Torneten for your friendship, mentorship, encouragement and inspiration. None of the good things in my life the past 18 years would have been possible without you.

I would like to think my editor Jeanne for her patience and diligence to detail- you have made a readable masterpiece from the rough draft. 😊

Thank you Jason Dickson for your insight and expertise when it comes to lending. You have stepped up when I needed your help and have been a tremendous support with this book.

I appreciate those people who have been with me through thick and thin through the years and Josh Bishop is one of those people for me. Josh is the architect of my web design and picture art on the covers and in the book. He is a genius at his craft and I cannot recommend him enough for his expertise in Design! Thank you for your friendship.

I would like to thank Dr. Hank at Agent Wealth Network for your friendship, mentorship and all the help you have given me. You are a real estate angel. Yeeeesss!

I would like to thank Michael Sandler at Inspire Nation. The education, perspective and guidance you have given me and my family are priceless. Woo hoo!

I would like to thank Mason Whitehead at Churchill Mortgage for your patience and with the details on the financing. Working with you is a joy and an honor as I have seen you work with integrity.

I would like to thank Duncan Campbell — you are a genius with numbers and accounting and infinitely patient as well as a true treasure as a CPA and business partner.

I would like to thank Nicole Andrews for your friendship and mentorship over the years- I would not be where I am in real estate today without you. Thank you.

I would like to thank Doug Mefford. You keep it real and keep me on my side of the street. Your friendship and support mean the world to me and my family — if you don't believe me just ask my wife.

To my dear friends in the Chicago Group — you are my lifeline and lifeblood. Through you and with you I learn how to do this life by principle.

To my parents and stepparents (Dennis, Angie, Patsy and Richard) and all my family and friends — my deepest thanks. You have always been in my corner cheering me on from games to school to life. I am so blessed to be surrounded by such wonderful amazing people.

To my amazing, beautiful wife Mercy for your support and dedication and my four kids: Chloe for her inspiration from above, Charles, Finnegan and the little one on the way — I love you.

And finally, to the reader — thank you for giving of your most precious resource: your time and attention to read this book. This book is for you. It was created to be of service to you. My prayer is that it will be so.

About the Author

Ryan is currently a Realtor in Dallas, TX and has been for the past 10 years. He is currently with the one of the fastest growing real estate brokerage firms in North America with more than 15,000 agents across 50 US States, The District of Columbia and three Canadian Provinces. As a publicly traded company, eXp World Holdings uniquely offers real estate professionals within its ranks opportunities to earn company stock for production and contributions to overall company growth. WooHoo!

Ryan is originally from Council Bluffs, Iowa. He attended college in LaCrosse, WI where he played college soccer and earned a degree in Marketing and Management at Viterbo University. He went on to become the assistant men's soccer coach at the University of Memphis and during his four years there, acquired his Masters in Sports Management. He then coached the Men's soccer program at Austin College.

Ryan is married to the lovely Mercy Shea and has three children: Chloe, Charles, and Finnegan. He now resides in Dallas, where he sells real estate and writes books on the real estate industry. You can find out more by going to www.CondoLivingDallas.com.

Made in the USA
Columbia, SC
23 February 2019